Cold Comfort

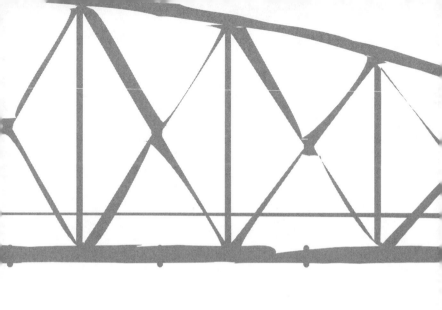

University of Minnesota Press Minneapolis • London

Cold Comfort

Life at the Top
of the Map

Barton Sutter

For permission information, see pages 209–10.

Published by the University of Minnesota Press
111 Third Avenue South, Suite 290
Minneapolis, MN 55401-2520
http://www.upress.umn.edu

Library of Congress Cataloging-in-Publication Data

Sutter, Barton, 1949–
Cold comfort : life at the top of the map / Sutter, Barton.
p.   cm.
ISBN 0-8166-3259-6 (hc : alk. paper)
1. Sutter, Barton, 1949–   — Homes and haunts — Minnesota —
Duluth.   2. Authors, American — 20th century — Biography.
3. Duluth (Minn.) — Social life and customs.   I. Title.
PS3569.U87Z464   1998
818'.5409
[B] — DC21
98-20337

Printed in the United States of America on acid-free paper

The University of Minnesota is an equal-opportunity educator
· and employer.

10 09 08 07 06 05 04 03 02 01 00 99
10 9 8 7 6 5 4 3

For
Dorothea,
Lilo,
and
Bettina

Contents

Acknowledgments

I remember swearing out loud, my first week in Duluth, as I walked the shining sand of Park Point — with waves crashing on the beach, sunlight flashing off wet pebbles, gulls crying curses at me from the sky — *"I'm going to write a book about this place!"*

Several years later, Liz Hannon, a producer for Minnesota Public Radio, actually got me going. Liz invited me to write a monthly essay for "Voices from the Heartland," a series she was starting for her "Midmorning" show. Before long I realized I was writing, month by month, the book about Duluth I had promised the sky that I would. So thanks, Liz. And thanks to all the friendly folks at MPR who helped me through the years.

In 1993 Minnesota Public Radio issued a limited edition audiocassette called *A Sense of Place*, which featured several of these pieces.

Many of these essays, originally written for radio, eventually appeared in periodicals, too, so I owe thanks to the editors who made room for my work in the pages of *The Boundary Waters Journal, Lake Country Journal, Minnesota Calls, Minnesota Monthly, Mpls.-St. Paul, NorthLife,* and the *UMD Statesman.*

John Henricksson published a group of these pieces under the collective title "Postcards from Duluth" in his anthology *North Writers II,* which was issued by the University of Minnesota Press in 1997.

Work on this book was also supported by an Individual Artist Fellowship from the Arrowhead Regional Arts Council.

Thanks to Margi Preus and the Duluth comedy troupe Colder by the Lake for inviting me to "perform" a number of these essays on their live radio shows, broadcast by KUMD. Those were hilarious opportunities.

Thanks to Warren Nelson and John Gustafson of the Lake Superior Big Top Chautauqua for inviting my brother and me to perform under the canvas and for later broadcasting parts of our show over Wisconsin Public Radio.

I owe a special debt to my friend Milan Kovacovic, who read every one of these essays and offered crucial criticism and encouragement.

Thanks to Todd Orjala at the University of Minnesota Press for believing in *Cold Comfort* and helping me put these essays in order. I'm also grateful to Linda Lincoln for close reading and astute suggestions.

I want to thank the members of the Duluth-Superior meeting of the Society of Friends, who helped me through hard times and deepened my appreciation for silence, well-chosen words, and hearty potluck dinners.

Thanks to my neighbors near Chester Creek and down on Park Point. Some are mentioned in this book and some are not, but many of them — in their daily acts of kindness and mutual aid, in their gossip and laughter — made the word *community* ring true for me again.

And thanks to all the friends, relatives, and strangers who offered stray words of interest and enthusiasm, fresh observations, and odd ideas. As I look back on the making of this book, it seems to me no truth is deeper than the deepest truth of ecology — that we are all related, that we are all, in reality, one.

I wrote these essays in and about the place where my mother grew up, but I see that it's my father's spirit that really haunts this book. His kindness, his love for the natural world and quirky people, his search for spiritual significance in the things of daily life, these are my rich inheritance; and he is my best, most encouraging ghost.

I owe my greatest thanks, always and forever, to my wife, Dorothea Diver, and to my stepdaughters, Lilo and Bettina Stuecher. They lived this book with me, and with them I am, finally, home.

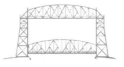

Homing

An Introduction

This book is about a place at the top of the map — a region ruled by water and snow, popple and pine, balsam and birch. North was always my favorite direction, and for years I longed to live up here in Duluth, on the shore of the largest lake in the world. After half a lifetime, I realized my desire.

Because my father was a minister, I moved, as a boy, from one tiny Midwestern town to another. So I grew up, like an army brat, with a vague but painful case of homesickness. My sense of homelessness was deepened, no doubt, by my mother's death when I was thirteen, but my homesickness was inherited, too. As the grandson of Scandinavian immigrants, I grew up hearing tales of the Old Country, that legendary land to which the elders of my family never returned. Most of us in this country probably suffer from a more-or-less constant, low-grade form of homesickness, but that ache may not be unique to Americans. A friend of mine, a professor of philosophy, once told me she thought the most fundamental question of all was whether humans could truly feel at home in the universe.

Duluth always felt like home to me, even when I was just passing through. My mother had grown up in this town, so my consciousness was colored by her stories, and my boyhood visits to her parents were lodged in my bones. My grandfather was a shipyard worker who chewed snoose and smelled of whiskey; his sinfulness intrigued me. My grandmother bubbled with stories about the twin ports of Duluth and Superior all the days of her very long life. As a child of the prairies, I found the hills of this lopsided city exciting, and Lake Superior fulfilled my fantasies about the ocean. The ore boats and foreign freighters seemed impossibly exotic. In Duluth, Canada felt very close, and the rumors I heard about the forests and canoe country up north fired my imagination. I had a kind of crush on this town. I liked the big sand beach at Park Point. I liked the old houses clinging to the hillside. I liked the white birch trees. I liked the very smell of this place — a bittersweet blend of industrial pollution and evergreens.

After my first year of college, I decided to quit and move to Duluth. I rented a room in a flophouse downtown and looked for work, but I couldn't find a job and had to abandon my plan. I kept returning to the area, though, and eventually lived for a year in an old fishing shack in Grand Marais, up near the Canadian border, working at a resort, in a bakery, on the local paper, scraping by. But then I got confused. I returned to college, graduated, and moved out to Boston, in a vain attempt to gain some urban sophistication. I did graduate

school in upstate New York. Failing to find the college
teaching job for which I had trained, I worked for a
year on a magazine in the bluff and river country of
southeastern Minnesota. Then I moved to Minneapolis,
where I worked as a swingshift typesetter for half a
dozen years. I married and moved to central Minnesota. I spent part of a year in Europe. But wherever
I went, a small insistent voice kept whispering, "Not it.
Not it. This isn't it."

Finally, at the age of thirty-seven, I decided place
was more important than employment. My wife had
earned a sabbatical, and I had won a modest fellowship.
For a year, we were free to live wherever we liked.
I liked Duluth, and my wife, who would be flying around
the country to do research in various libraries, agreed.

Those first few weeks in Duluth, I was euphoric.
I walked the hardwood floors of our apartment and stood
before the big window, gazing out at the blue expanse
of Lake Superior, my fists raised in triumph. Normally
rather reticent, I found myself speaking to strangers.
Normally somewhat solitary, I made friends easily.
I bought a canoe and began exploring the inland lakes
close to town. I started fishing with a vengeance. I took
trips into the Boundary Waters Canoe Area, the million-
acre wilderness that begins just two hours north of
Duluth. Something strange was happening. I seemed to
be happy here, even though I had gradually grown to
believe that happiness was a shallow emotion reserved
for people who lacked brains.

When that first year in Duluth was up, I refused to
leave. I found a part-time teaching job, and my wife,
who had fallen for northern Minnesota, too, arranged

her schedule so she could commute back home to Duluth for long weekends. We managed this divided life, with summers together, for several years; but our marriage, which had already weakened, snapped under the strain. The year I turned forty I sold a book of stories to a major publisher, I won a substantial fellowship, and my personal life blew apart. My marriage was over. I was an alcoholic. I was in love. My dreams crackled with crazy, mythic imagery, and I woke to find myself caught in a classic midlife crisis.

But this book is not a confession of sordid secrets. I can't compete with the TV talk shows, nor do I wish to. This book is about a place, the city of Duluth and the Arrowhead region of Minnesota — a place that saved my life. Or so it seems these days. For, looking back, I'm not at all certain I would have survived my midlife passage — the bewilderment and confusion, the guilt and anger, the suicidal flashes — if I had been living anywhere else. As dark as those days were, I still wanted, every day, to see what the light looked like on Lake Superior. This place, which had drawn me back to it with magnetic force all my life, pulled me through. These essays are, at least in part, expressions of my gratitude.

One hesitates, here at the close of the twentieth century, to publish anything in praise of place. Humans are so numerous now, we can overrun a good place as soon as the word gets out. So from time to time, writing these essays, I've suffered attacks of anxiety. But my worries have always evaporated in laughter. Who would want to move to a place where the temperature can drop to forty below? Although our summers are dangerously seductive, we are saved, up here on the northern rim, by our crummy economy; by our practical, unfashionable clothes; and, most of all, by the cold — the ferocious, unfathomable cold. As Duluthians like to say, it keeps the riffraff out.

In any case, this book is no travel brochure. Call it a lover's quarrel with a peculiar place, the record of one man's homecoming. Many Americans live with a sense of exile and seek, half-consciously, a place to heal that hurt. Northern Minnesota can cure that ache for very few. It's just too cold and provincial up here. I'm not expecting company. But I would be pleased if this book not only entertained you, restless reader, but pointed the way to some odd, forsaken place that makes the tuning fork beneath *your* breastbone hum.

January 13, 1998
Duluth, Minnesota
21 below zero

ONE LOPSIDED CITY

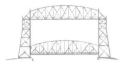

Dull and Out of It

I live in Duluth, and I've got reasons. Lake Superior is a big one. Twenty-three streams running through town are twenty-three more. The largest natural sandbar in the world is another. And I'm tickled to live in a city where bears wander the streets every fall like country cousins come to town to see the sights.

Duluth has its cultural attractions, too — everything from a symphony orchestra to one of the best Greek restaurants in Minnesota. Yet I have the impression that many people, if they think of this city at all, consider Duluth a cold kind of joke, a Peoria of the North, the last outpost on the northernmost edge of the middle of nowhere.

One summer evening I was discussing this view of Duluth with my friend Roger, who moved here more than twenty years ago. We were sitting under an umbrella at a place that sells imported beers. "It's true," Roger grinned. "My relatives back in Kentucky still think of Duluth as a military base, some sort of radar station. They think we all live in Quonsets." We laughed and turned to watch a foreign freighter float off through the moonlight on Lake Superior. I would add to all the other pleasures of this place the sweet and luxurious feeling of being underestimated and mis- understood.

Quite a few Duluthians, I've discovered, actually glory in this image of backwardness and do all they can to promote it, hoping, perhaps, to keep the hordes of tourists at bay. It's not unusual for natives to badmouth this town to outsiders, though I've noticed that the talk about terrible winters is often delivered with a sly smile. A few years back the city put out bumper stickers that declared: "We're Duluth and proud of it." I saw one sticker that was customized to read: "We're Dull and out of it." Duluthians enjoy being out of the swim, and that's not just a metaphor. Lake Superior, the city's main attraction, remains too frigid for swimming for all but a couple of weeks of the year.

Duluth is hardly the little town that time forgot. This is a city of a hundred thousand odd souls, and some of them are lost. As in any other urban area in America, crooked politics, murder, racism, and rape are all committed here. It's impossible to get too dewy- eyed about this place.

But there are pleasures to be had in a city like Duluth — and in Peoria, too, I imagine — that are unavailable to the residents of fancier towns. There's the pleasure of helping strangers push their car out of a snowdrift. There's the true sense of security that comes from knowing you can leave your doors unlocked.

There's the gigantic surprise of noticing a moose in the yard across the street. There's the deep satisfaction of yelling at your neighbors' kids as if they were your own.

Among the most relaxing of these many pleasures, though, is the confidence that comes from knowing what you're not. These epiphanies are most likely to occur in January, when your car heater is blasting drafts of air that feel like August in Missouri and you're swaddled up in goose down, mukluks, and a bomber cap with fur earflaps. Driving down Superior Street on a Saturday night, the sidewalks deserted, wind off the lake blowing snow through the pink light from the street lamps, the temperature stuck at twenty below, you know this isn't Paris. This isn't even Minneapolis. This is Duluth. You feel the truth of that.

Consequently, you can forget about the latest trends. No need to worry, up here, about which brand of mustard is most fashionable these days. If you want a slice of lemon in your water glass, you'll have to special order that. But you can get by with jeans and a flannel shirt in even the snazziest restaurant. In that regard, life in Duluth is a great relief. And if lack of style sometimes amounts to a kind of pugnacious style itself, it's one that, personally, I find fatally attractive. I'm Duluth and proud of it. I'm Dull and out of it.

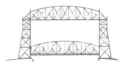

"A Citty upon a Hill"

In 1630, bound for Massachusetts Bay, John Winthrop preached a sermon in which he declared to his fellow Puritans: "wee shall be as a Citty upon a Hill." And some politician in every damn American election ever since has felt compelled to quote him, insisting that the nation ought to be a city on a hill. If we put that proposal into action, it would generate a lot of jobs — especially in the flatlands of Kansas and Nebraska — but of course our candidate doesn't mean for us to actually crank up the dozers and start moving dirt. No, he's just talking, as politicians will, meaning to imply that the U.S. — us — we ought to set some sort of spiritual and moral example for the world. But I don't trust this tired metaphor. Here in Duluth, we are not just *as* a Citty upon a Hill, we *are* a Citty upon a Hill, and a Citty upon a Hill has its downside, let me tell you.

Oh, the view is absolutely stupendous, no doubt about that. When my parents first brought me here as a kid, and Lake Superior opened out in front of me like an ocean, I lost my breath. I haven't quite got it back yet. Still today, when I drive in from the south, and the freeway lifts me over Thompson Hill, I hyperventilate. The hills of Duluth mark the beginning of the most crinkly country in Minnesota. Cartographers call these ups and downs *relief,* and that's what I feel whenever I return to Duluth, relief at having escaped the monotony of the plains that dominate most of the state. Whenever I feel cramped by daily duties, I can take a quick trip along Skyline Drive, the road that rides the ridgeline for twenty miles through town. Or I can visit my pal Steve, who owns a little hilltop house with about the best view in all of Duluth. His house is far from fancy, but Steve can stand on his front stoop, the pauper prince of all he surveys, and observe the lower reaches of the St. Louis River, watch the tugboats nudge a freighter through the harbor, mark the long, blue line of Minnesota's North Shore, look away to the green hills of Wisconsin, and try, at the far, hazy edge of the world, to separate sky from sweetwater sea. The view from this great hump of granite and basalt is downright thrilling, even spiritually uplifting, but I can't say I've seen much evidence that Duluthians derive any real moral benefit from living on a hill.

The one virtue Duluthians possess to a larger degree than other citizens of Minnesota — a state in which caution is a byword anyway, a state whose official motto ought to be "We'll see" — the one virtue on which Duluthians have an absolute lock is prudence. Natives are taught from birth to set the emergency brake and turn their wheels to the curb. Duluthians also know there are certain things you simply do not do. You don't mess with the winding streets of Little Italy in a blizzard. You don't go near Goat Hill all winter. And unless you're really, really bored, you don't turn down Nineteenth Avenue East in a sleetstorm. Visitors take one look at Lake Avenue, which we used for a downhill ski race a couple years back, and wonder out loud how we drive this town in winter. I tell you, there's a weird satisfaction in seeing that the very streets of your city strike terror in a stranger's heart. But our secret is relatively simple: we stay home a lot. My grandparents, who spent most of their lives in West Duluth, had some very good friends who lived on the Heights. In order to visit them, my grandparents had to drive up Piedmont Avenue, which used to have a rope strung along the sidewalk so pedestrians could haul themselves uphill. "In winter," my grandmother explained, "we never saw those people."

Now, I believe in caution. I'm Scandinavian, after all, and I choose to live in this lopsided town where we've perfected the Minnesota Shuffle — that babystep technique that keeps you from knockin' your noggin on the ice. But prudence, the only virtue at which we actually excel in this particular city on a hill, strikes me as an awfully odd rallying cry. It's sort of boring, isn't it? And prudence has a dark side, too, as we're highly aware up here where ambition tends to be stymied by our belief that life is precarious and everything is going downhill.

"A Citty upon a Hill"

So the next time you hear a politician say we ought to be a city on a hill, ask him if he's ever been one. Better yet, offer him a ticket to Duluth. We like tourists, and we're served by a major airline, whenever the weather permits.

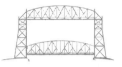

The Bridge

For three cold months each year, the Aerial Lift Bridge stands unmoving on the frozen shore of Lake Superior, like a giant metal sculpture. Here on the northern edge of the known universe, robins are unreliable, tulips freeze overnight, and April showers turn to snow more often than to flowers. But once the lift bridge begins to rise and fall, allowing ships and ore boats to slip through the canal, we know we're connected to the rest of the world by water again, and we can safely expect some sort of summer before too awfully long.

Bridges are to Duluth what skyscrapers are to New York. They define the place. We've got the Bong. We've got the Blatnik. We've got trestles and docks and piers. We've even got a road called Seven Bridges. But the queen of them all, without doubt, is the Aerial Lift Bridge. Neither the longest nor the highest bridge in town, the Lift is merely the oldest and the loveliest.

Modeled after a bridge in France, the Lift began life back in 1905 as the Aerial Ferry Bridge. A carriage suspended from a steel framework carried passengers back and forth across the ship canal, which had been dug through Park Point some thirty years before. In 1929 the transfer car was replaced by a movable steel span, and the bridge became the literal gateway to the harbor that we know today.

Wonderfully old-fashioned, graceful, light, and airy, the lift bridge is a pleasure to behold and, over the years, has come to serve as a symbol for the city. It's our unofficial logo, and we duplicate it shamelessly — on flyers and brochures, on keychains, coffee mugs, and placemats — as if to say: This Bridge R Us. And in some strange way, it is. Location has a lot to do with that. The bridge is a kind of crossroads. Not only does it function as a gate between the harbor and Lake Superior but also as an entrance to Park Point, the longest freshwater sandbar in the world. What's more, Lake Avenue, which runs across the bridge, divides Duluth in half, east from west. The lift bridge stands at the center of the city, a sort of X that marks the most important spot in town.

I drove down to the bridge the other day and hit it lucky. A Canadian steamship was just heading out of the harbor, so I got to watch the span go up as the concrete counterweights, as large as cars, came down, and the big black boat, as impressive as a grand hotel, trailing a veil of smoke from her stack, eased beneath the bridge and out to sea.

That was a sight, for sure, but this visit reminded me there's as much to hear as to see down at the ship canal:

the catcalls of gulls, the swash and smack of waves
against the piers, and then, as the boat approaches, the
low, hoarse groan of her horn — *long, short, short* — and
immediately, the higher-pitched response from the
pilot house of the bridge — *long, short, short.* These horns
are magnificent, really loud, even somewhat frightening. But there's also the trill of the bell that warns
pedestrians to clear the bridge. And finally, once the
span descends and traffic resumes, the hum of rubber
tires on the metal grating of the roadbed. This rich tex-
ture of sound is so suggestive it can drive people
slightly batty. My brother, a musician, spent an hour
listening to the bridge one foggy night and came away
with the lunatic desire to compose an orchestral piece
called *Suite for Male Chorus, Triangle, and Aerial Lift Bridge* —
a daringly innovative work that, I am sorry to report,
remains unwritten at this date.

The awful truth Duluthians refuse to face is that the
lift bridge is a preposterous anachronism. During the
shipping season, Park Point residents get held up
repeatedly by marine traffic passing through the ship
canal. Cars back up and tempers rise right along with
the roadbed of the bridge. This situation has spawned
a verb that may well be unique to the city of Duluth.
To be "bridged" means to be delayed by the rise of an
aerial lift bridge. As in, "Sorry I'm late. I left the house
at eight, but I got bridged." Any structure so trouble-
some that it causes alterations in the English language
ought to be replaced by something more efficient —
something large, concrete, and ugly. But I feel confident Duluthians would burn the mayor's house and
drown the city council in the ship canal before they'd

let that happen. This old latticework of steel and sky is as important to Duluth as the Eiffel Tower is to Paris. The affection that city residents demonstrate for this impractical piece of architecture gives me great hope. It could be an early sign of true culture here on the northern rim of noplace in particular. If we can feel affection and respect for a *bridge* — who knows? Someday we might even feel as much for nature or, impossible as it might seem, each other.

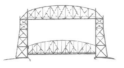

God

Having lived for several years beside "the shining big sea water," I've decided that Lake Superior is God. Does that seem blasphemous? Any human view of God is bound to be imperfect, but, the way I see it, the image of Lake Superior is a lot less insulting to the Supreme Being than the more conventional picture of a graybeard in bathrobe and sandals.

If I remember right, Anselm was the saint who defined God as "that being than which no greater can be conceived." Well, I can't conceive of any being greater than Lake Superior. The ocean, the sky, the sun, the northern lights, the Milky Way — these are plenty great enough, but, to my mind anyway, they're all too distant and amorphous to truly qualify as beings. I saw a mountain in Norway once that seemed pretty great. I looked out the window of the train, and here was this tremendous . . . *being*. That great white rocky mountain looked alive; it seemed to pulsate, as if it had a heart; it spoke to me, and this is what the mountain said: *"I am big, and you are very small."* That mountain was probably God, but I only saw it once, and that was long ago and far away. We need our gods nearby. The ancient Greeks knew that. I live less than a mile from the greatest of all the Great Lakes, which is, for me, "that being than which no greater can be conceived."

To tell the truth, I've lived most of my adult life as a fairly arrogant agnostic. The existence of God seemed to depend on my mood. If things were going badly, then there was no God, and, besides, He was a gigantic Jerk. If things were to my liking, my inner world felt a lot like Johnny Mathis singing "Misty," and I thought maybe God was everywhere but just invisible, like oxygen. I might have gone on, more or less content with my childish theology, except that I discovered, in the middle of my life, that such vague attitudes were harmful to my health. Apparently I'm like a Russian peasant: I have to have an icon. Without a clear image of God, my free-floating spiritual desire is apt to attach itself to the wrong object. I mean, I'm completely capable of thinking beer is God. Or sex is God. Or money. Or, hey, maybe *I'm* God! The world is full of dumb ideas, and half of them pass through my head each day. In order to protect myself from the more dangerous ones, I've decided Lake Superior is God.

I didn't come to this decision overnight. A quarter of a century ago, when I was in my early teens, my family stopped one evening in Duluth, and I ran down to skip rocks off the silver surface of Superior, to watch the water darken and go black. Gazing out over that great body of water, dizzied by the incense of spruce and

Balm of Gilead, I had what the psychologists call "an oceanic experience." This might be described as a semi-mystical state in which time slows down to zero and the boundaries of the self dissolve. To put it very poorly, I felt one with the universe. I felt grief, relief, melancholy, peace, and excitement all at once. Whatever that experience was in fact, it felt religious, and Lake Superior has been sacred to me ever since. Before I got married, I took a week and made a solo drive all the way around the lake. Ten years later, in the agony of separation and divorce, I drove down to the lake in desperation several times a day for days on end, as if that great sweetwater sea could heal me. And it did. Or nearly.

But I didn't know that I considered Lake Superior God until a couple of years ago. One of the many pleasures of living in Duluth is that you have to look at the lake a lot. You might only mean to get some groceries or a hammer from the hardware store, but on your way you see something so grand, so terrible and beautiful, that you absorb your daily requirement of humility just by driving down the street. I've also found that the sight of Lake Superior works very well to shock me out of self-pity, a state of mindlessness to which I seem to be especially prone. I was deep in such a funk the night I finally realized that the lake was God.

I was driving home from the local shopping mall, where, once again, life had failed to fulfill my fantasies. Malls are all I need to know of hell, but I had eagerly agreed to go to hell because I had recently published a book, a book that represented my best efforts on this earth. So for two gruesome hours I had sat in a generic

bookstore, like a kid at a Kool-aid stand, smiling nicely
at hundreds of people who looked right through me.
I had sold and signed one book. Sick with shame, mut-
tering murderous ideas, I topped the hill above the city
and saw, straight ahead, the biggest, most gorgeous
moon I'd ever witnessed in my life and there, below it,
royal purple glinting gold from here to the edge of the
world, Lake Superior. Only I didn't say, "Lake Superior!"
I didn't say, "What a view!" I didn't say, "How beautiful!"
No, no, no. Immediately, instinctively, I gave the lake
its proper name. What I said was: "God!"

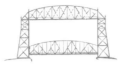

Park Point

The majority of tourists who visit Duluth manage to locate the ship canal and the Aerial Lift Bridge, but many of them miss Park Point, the most remarkable feature of the city. Too bad. It's easy enough to find. All you have to do to drive down the length of it is cross the lift bridge. Park Point (also known as Minnesota Point) is both a geographic feature and a neighborhood, the only true beach community in the entire state.

Essentially one tremendous sandbar, Park Point was formed by the waves of Lake Superior colliding with the currents of the Nemadji and St. Louis rivers. The Point stretches out into the lake for seven miles, breaks for a natural canal, and then continues, as Wisconsin Point, for three more miles to the mainland. This is the longest freshwater sandbar in the world, and it creates, on the landward side, the calm waters of the Duluth Harbor and Superior Bay.

Unusual physical features are naturally attractive. The Ojibway used to camp on Park Point, and Daniel Greysolon Sieur du Lhut landed here in 1679. The Point was officially a village by the middle of the nineteenth century, and in 1889 it was added to the city of Duluth. Duluth is long and narrow anyhow, but Park Point — only two blocks wide — qualifies as the skinniest neighborhood in town. Most of the houses cling to either side of Minnesota Avenue, the one through street, which stops at Sky Harbor, an airport for private planes, five miles down the Point. Along the way, there's a Coast Guard station and marina, a rowing club, a grocery store, a fire hall, and two small churches, Our Lady of Mercy and St. Andrews By-the-Lake. Not a lot of business is done down here. Park Point is basically the city's sandbox.

Newcomers to Duluth almost always look for housing on Park Point, it's that romantic. I've been drawn to the area since I was a kid. But I've also lived in Duluth long enough to be wary of the drawbacks. The Point is like an island. The only access by car is across the Aerial Lift Bridge, and this means Park Pointers spend hours of their lives each year waiting for boats to pass beneath the bridge so the span can be lowered so they can get on or off the Point. On the sweetest summer days the traffic backs up because everyone in town wants to be on the beach. In winter the worst winds come blasting out of the northeast, unchecked for three hundred miles, roaring down the length of Lake Superior to rattle the windows and rip shingles off the roof. Who needs that? I asked myself, after my divorce. I was selling my house and hunting for a studio.

A friend was moving out of his tiny duplex on Park
Point and wanted to know if I would be interested.
The Point has grown so fashionable, and I'm so ornery,
I almost said no. Luckily, my friends know what's good
for me better than I know myself. They convinced me
I'd be crazy not to take the place.

And so I did. I felt pretty temporary there at first.
I was out of town a lot and still reeling from the process
of selling my house and moving out. When it comes to
stress, psychologists rank the purchase or sale of a
house right behind divorce and the death of a spouse.
I gave myself a year to adjust to life on the Point. Still,
it seemed odd that I couldn't settle right in. After all,
I was living a boyhood fantasy. The studio was cozy, my
neighbors were friendly, and a hundred yards out the
door a sand dune rose up twenty-five feet and spilled
down to the beach and the great blue lake, which
opened out toward Wisconsin, the North Shore,
Canada, farther than I could see. Maybe this was just
too terrific to be true.

Along about the end of August, when summer finally
arrived in Duluth, I began to feel at home. One day the
temperature broke ninety — a rare phenomenon around
here — and half the city quit work to come sit on the
sand. Not only was the water warm enough for swimming, it was downright pleasant, something that only
happens about two days out of a very good year. In a
mile-long stretch of beach, I met a dozen acquaintances
from various parts of town. People came and went all
day, and with my place serving as a parking lot, pop
stand, changing room, and potty stop, my prestige
and popularity zoomed. Somebody brought chicken,

somebody brought beer. A quarter moon appeared. The wind shifted just in time and blew the bugs away. More friends arrived, sank in a heap on the sand, and began to harmonize. I gathered driftwood with the kids and built a bonfire bright as a blast furnace. We stayed there, staring cross-eyed at the fire, till we grew so woozy we had to head for bed.

The next morning when I checked the beach, there wasn't a soul in sight. The empty, glittering shoreline stretched away for miles, and it seemed to belong to me.

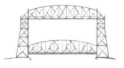

Sister City

Here in Duluth we tend to be a little earnest about our civic responsibilities. Take our sister city program. The last time I checked, we had not one but four official sister cities: Thunder Bay, Ontario; Växjö, Sweden; Ōhara, Japan; and a city in Russia that sounds like a brand of vodka made out of diesel fuel, Petrozavodsk. As if this weren't enough, a delegation has gone off to Cuba, and there's been talk of sending out a search party to look for a compatible town somewhere in South America. Do we really need any more sister cities? How about a couple of brother cities? How about a daddy city? Or maybe a grandma city?

Actually, I think the sister city concept is a fine idea and really does what it's supposed to do — promote peace and understanding. I just doubt we need a different city for every man, woman, and child in Duluth. And I remain somewhat skeptical of all this international affection. I know that it's far easier to romanticize a sibling who lives halfway 'round the world than one who lives nearby. Anyone can fall in love with Växjö or Ōhara. But who cares about Superior, Wisconsin?

Although the relationship is unofficial, Superior is Duluth's one-and-only, down-and-dirty, honest-to-goodness sister city. Like Fargo and Moorhead, like Fort Frances and International Falls, like Minneapolis and St. Paul, Duluth and Superior are twin towns divided by water — in this case, the St. Louis River and the splendid harbor at its mouth. On almost every point, Superior suffers by comparison. Duluth has 90,000 inhabitants; Superior, 30,000. Duluth has some of the most impressive nineteenth-century architecture in the Midwest; Superior is famous for asphalt shingles and insulbrick. Duluth is known for first-rate medical facilities; Superior has an oil refinery. Duluth has Spirit Mountain and a ski jump; Superior is flat as a turkey platter. Superior is clearly inferior to Duluth, but if you like an underdog, you have to love that town across the harbor. I sure do.

Superior, as I see it, is absolute ground zero. If you can survive with some joy in that city of rust and despair, you can hang on anywhere. I like to test visitors by driving them over the High Bridge to see how they react to such a busted place. I like to scare myself by driving around over there, especially in midwinter, when the sky is the same dirty gray as the streets. At that time of year it feels like the grimmest place on the face of the earth. Oddly enough, I find such conditions inspiring. Superior in March is to me what Tahiti was to Gauguin. As I cruise past the boarded-up buildings and flashing bar signs on Tower Avenue, I find myself asking the same large questions that crazy painter had to go to paradise to ask: "Who are we? Why are we here? Where are we going?"

My grandparents liked to think of themselves as residents of Duluth but actually spent a large part of their lives in Superior. When times were fat, they lived in Duluth. When times got lean (more often than not), they moved to Superior and survived. Things were cheaper over there. They still are. My grandfather worked in the shipyards of Superior and could get us onto the boats. I felt as if he owned the city, but of course he didn't. He didn't own a house. He did own — once, briefly, with the bank — a tiny gas station ("Biggest Li'l Station in Town"), but he gave his customers too much credit and lost his shirt. My grandfather drank too much, too — an easy thing to do in Superior. When he died, he was living alone in the Ryan Hotel, which, along with my grandfather, has vanished from the earth, though the place glimmered once, even in its run-down days, with a card room, a café, and a bar that blushed pink neon. How could I not love the city in which one of my favorite people chose to die? I do, as you might love a sister who dropped out of school, married badly, and always shows up in hand-me-down clothes: bruised, broken, but, as Faulkner might say, unvanquished.

Superior has been permanently caught in the Great Depression, but by now the depression is more profound than economics, deeper than psychology. This is the city where the Great Lakes ore boats go to die. Their rusting hulks lie stranded on the waterfront, waiting to be scrapped. It's a railroad town, too, the end of the line, where boxcars come to rest. This place is so desperate the residents recently built a new library inside a former supermarket. For a while Superior had an energetic young mayor who did his best to revive the city; one night some ungrateful citizen tried to burn his house. It's a town of stunted trees and cracked sidewalks, of bitterness and broken windows.

No wonder, then, that in Superior, alcohol, that all-purpose painkiller, is king. The town is famous for its bars, where you can still buy beer for a quarter a glass and Everclear to go. These are the friendliest taverns on earth — dangerous and warm — where the denizens sit hunched around their hearts, which hurt from life at twelve below zero, from gazing all day at the glittering hills of Duluth.

But there is poetry in this mecca of despair, this provincial capital of desolation. Let me praise the city of Superior by reciting her signs, which sound to me like sobs, or cries for help, or a lonesome song: Mike's Place, the Cedar Lounge, Lost in the 50's, Kady's Whirlpool/Sauna/Massage, Betty Boop's, Molly's, Anchor Bar, Tyomies Finnish American Bookstore, Jesus/the way, the truth, the life/Come into my heart Lord Jesus, Pink Cadillac, girls girls exotic dancers, Cove Cabaret Night Club, Red Wing Shoes, the Metal Shop, LaBelle, BINGO, Palace Theatre, VICTORY FELLOWSHIP, Popeye, the Locker Room, Capri, Bob's Chop Suey House, Frankie's, the Dugout, Elbo Room, Globe News.

O, sad, sweet Superior! Sister city!

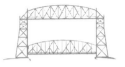

April Fools

Here in Duluth, April lasts about eight weeks. It starts in late March and drags on until, oh, say, the fishing opener in mid-May. April is both the longest and the meanest month of the year. Sure, January can be shocking, with subzero temps, but at least you're braced for that. At least you can ski. What's April good for? This nasty season will dazzle you with sunshine for a couple of hours now and then, but the minute you take off your shirt, the weather turns to seven days of sleet followed by dirty fog followed by a blizzard. And that's not the worst of it. The worst of it is knowing that those undeserving city slickers down in Minneapolis are already sniffing lilacs.

The problem with Duluth in April is that great big lake in our front yard. At an almost constant thirty-nine degrees, Lake Superior moderates the vicious winter temperatures somewhat and acts as a splendid air conditioner in August. But the great lake also keeps us cool in April, eliminating spring, condemning us instead to mist and mud and drizzle. If Duluth were truly urban, lousy weather might not make much difference. But this is really just an oversized town, geared to outdoor activities. When the weather turns dreary, about all you can do for fun around here is go to the library.

So. How to survive this period in purgatory, this season of sludge and depression. The lucky among us — the wealthy and wise — get away. Having resisted the vacation fever that hits Duluth in February, having saved their funds for the desolate days of April, now, at last, when the landscape looks about as colorful as meatloaf, they leave — for the Cayman Islands, for Miami and Santa Fe, for Des Moines, Owatonna, Blaine — anywhere that might be warmer than Duluth. The sissies.

Those of us left behind turn green with envy — which is more than you can say for the grass around here. Left behind, forced to rely on our own ingenuity, we are the real April fools. Some of our survival tactics may seem rather desperate, but here are a half-dozen ritualistic activities you might be driven to try if you were stuck in Duluth during this dreary month.

1. You can pick up gum wrappers and pop cans revealed by the retreating snow. This activity seems to be especially favored by the very old and the very young, but anyone can do it.

2. Hack branches off a bush, place them in a vase with water, and watch to see if they leaf out. It helps to decorate the twigs with tinfoil and feathers . . . if you can find any.

3. Hose old dog dung off the sidewalk. A service to the whole community.

4. Take the kids to a greenhouse so they can be reminded of the jungly smell of summer and see what flowers look like. After the field trip, the children may want to make their own flowers from construction paper. They can tape these to the windows if the frost isn't too thick.

5. Drive to Hinckley to see if the trees have budded out down there. Even if they haven't, you can get a caramel roll out of the deal.

6. Throw off your Midwestern inhibitions and go shopping for some gaudy clothes. Or, if you just can't bring yourself to pay good money for anything so friv- olous, borrow a deer hunting outfit and wear blaze orange for a week or so.

There are other techniques, like hotel swimming parties and parka picnics, but they're really too pathetic to outline in detail.

I will say the most important skill for a Duluthian this time of year is the ability to avoid visitors. Normally we glory in tourism, but April is a dirty secret we try not to mention. A couple years back my cousin Lennart from Sweden dropped in out of the blue . . . or, I should say, out of the gray. Lennart is famous for showing up without warning. In fact, my brother made up a knock-knock joke about him. Goes like this: "Knock, knock." "Who's there?" "Lennart." Anyway, Lennart showed up one gray April day, and I got all excited. I'm obnoxiously proud of this dirty old town, and here was a chance to impress a relative from the

Old Country. Alas, we were socked in with fog and
sleet during his entire visit. Desperate, I drove Lennart
down to Park Point, where we stumbled over glacial
mounds of ice and listened to the foghorn groan like
Paul Bunyan with a bellyache. I have a few photos of
that afternoon. There's Lennart, dressed in a yellow
slicker, holding a scarlet umbrella, standing in an ice
field, enveloped by clouds of fog. It looks like a scene
from Venus, or Antarctica, or a Fellini movie, but it's
just an ordinary April in Duluth.

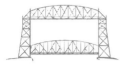

Tischer Creek

The other day I went out to see if Tischer Creek was still there after the long, harsh winter. Well, it was, thank goodness. The creek was up and running hard, burbling and yakking and rushing headlong down the dozens of waterfalls, large and small, that decorate its length as it drops toward Lake Superior. The sky was blue, the sun was warm, and the air was spiced with the incense of balsam and pine. After loitering along the creek for an hour, I could head back to the office, reassured somehow that the world was still in working order.

Tischer Creek is one of my favorite places in all of Duluth. Twenty-three streams run down through this town to the lake — that's about one every mile — but Tischer is the one I think of as mine. That's odd. I live right next to Chester Creek, which is bigger and far more dramatic. There's a place on Chester Creek, where, almost any summer day, you can watch brave boys, driven mad by sunshine and testosterone, leap off a thirty-foot bluff into a plunge pool below. That's always fun. And I love the Lester River, dark and sweet-scented, with broad, black pools, where I caught so many rainbow trout the first year I moved here. But Tischer Creek remains my favorite.

"Nature loves to hide," said Emerson, and it may be that I'm so fond of Tischer Creek because it's half-hidden and often overlooked. A wooden sign up from the bridge on Superior Street is the only hint the city offers, and that's pretty easy to miss. The tourists are all preoccupied with Lake Superior, which is pretty hard to miss, and Duluthians have so many other attractions to choose from that most days when I walk along Tischer Creek I get the whole ravine to myself.

A road runs alongside the creek, but it's blocked by a padlocked gate. I park the car beneath a big white pine and step out into the sound of the stream, which is like wind through the trees or waves breaking up on a beach, only different. This white noise is both varied and constant, and I will live in it until I leave the creek. The land that borders the creek, three-quarters of a mile from Superior Street to Vermillion Road, was donated by Chester Congdon in 1908, and the city — out of laziness or wisdom (sometimes they're the same) — has done precious little to improve it. How can you improve what's perfect? A gravel hiking trail parallels the creek about thirty feet back from the water. Otherwise, the place is just itself, a miniature wilderness smack in the middle of the city.

Modesty, I've come to see, is part of Tischer Creek's appeal. Living in Duluth, you get to look at Lake

Superior every day; the long view gives perspective and opens the mind. But Tischer Creek is intimate, encouraging those reveries that panoramas tend to wipe away. Here and there, the water widens into pools, but generally it looks as if a good broad jump would carry you across. The creek has all the features of a wild river — rapids, kettles, cataracts — it's just that they're small scale.

If the place itself is modest, so are my expectations. I don't come here looking to see a moose. The wildest animal I've ever encountered in this ravine is a crabby red squirrel. I might see a sharp-shinned hawk shoot through the trees, but that would be exceptional. Normally, I have to be satisfied with watching water-striders do their tricks and witnessing the tiny flowers for which I have no names. This morning, I'm surprised by a lowly toad, bumping slowly along the trail, like a living lump of mud. I'm told there are brook trout in Tischer Creek, but I've never seen more than a minnow, and I've never bothered to bring a rod. Why should I? I don't want a thing out of Tischer Creek — not a fish, not a stone. It's just that every once in a while I need to be here.

The bedrock at the lower end of Tischer Creek, where I begin my walk, is feldspar — a soft, volcanic rock the creek has cut through like a liquid saw. Because this rock resembles human flesh, ranging in color from pink to red, the ravine always feels rather eerie here. As I move along the trail, I turn aside from time to time on paths that go right to the edge of the stream. People have naturally worn these paths to their favorite sites along the creek. These places are like stations-of-the-cross for pagans, and I pause at most of them. Here, for instance, I can step out on a little bluff beneath some big red pines and watch whitewater come rocketing down a redrock sluice and turn dark in the pool at my feet. There the foam on the surface swirls round in a pattern as attractive as the marbled endpapers you find in old, expensive books.

When I cross over Fourth Street, the bedrock turns black, a heavier, harder form of lava than the feldspar downstream. There are even more rapids and falls up here. And here's an especially sweet spot where I just have to stop and sit for a while. A big old willow leans over the stream, and its lines are so pleasing it looks like a kind of calligraphy. How the eye loves to follow a curve or zigzag. How interesting this crooked creek compared to any drainage ditch. Here water slips over a slanting ledge, pools, and cuts back the other way like a lesson in composition. Below the willow, beside the ledge, the mosses grow, both green and red. Here is the place, I tell myself, to bring your troubled mind. Here is the very place, I think, to just quit thinking altogether, watch the stream go by but stay but rush right past but still remain, giving off a sound like thunder, rain, and tiny bells.

When I hit Vermillion Road, I turn and hurry back down the trail, ignoring those places where I lingered before. I'm running out of time, and I've saved the best for last. Instead of heading up to the car, I leave the main trail and follow a rocky path right beside the creek until the ravine becomes a canyon with walls a hundred feet high. I'm lost in shadows now but come around a bend, and there's a surprise — a footbridge with railings, arching over the stream, as if it had grown right out of the rock. Further downstream there's another, and another: three bridges altogether, like reflections of each other. When I cross the last bridge, I'm standing on the canyon floor. I know I'm in Duluth, but I feel I'm somewhere else — Montana or Japan. The floor of the canyon is an alluvial fan of fine brown sand. I rest in the shade of a grand old willow while the creek curves away and flashes in the sun before it disappears in a tangle of brush. I visited Tischer Creek a half-dozen times before I discovered her deepest secret. This is a place apart down here. The canyon has a mythic atmosphere. It's easy to imagine how a people might have made this womblike space their tribal source, the center of the earth from which the original folk went forth. Pleased to be here, I gaze up and up at the raw red walls, which are hung with cedars and little waterfalls that shatter in the sunlight.

As I climb up from the canyon to the car, I realize Tischer Creek has helped me see the difference between the things I think I want and what I really need, a distinction that seems to grow more crucial as we age. I'm absolutely crazy, for example, about the northern landscape. I'd like to buy the Boundary Waters. I'd like to own Alaska and kick everybody out except a couple friends. That's what I want. That's the size of my desire. But what I really need is to visit Tischer Creek now and again. I've read about a place in Russia where, every year, the locals contemplate certain sacred icons with such intensity that they are able to walk barefoot through fire. Tischer Creek does something similar for me. I come here, not to think, but to wash away my worries, to rid myself of all my best ideas and fill up instead on images — dew in the grass, a bug on the water, sunshine on red rock — pictures to sustain me when I go back to the world of cinder block and fluorescent lights where most of us work these days. Stuck with high-tech ugliness, I listen for the whisper of a stream called Tischer Creek.

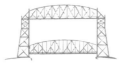

Ghost of a Good Bad Man

W hen the grass turns green at last, the residents of Duluth grow giddy, throw their windows open to the sweet, new air, and, stirred by a wild urge for renewal, set about spring cleaning. One year, I went completely radical. Instead of just sweeping, scrubbing, and painting, I decided to move out altogether.

It's not that I'd wrecked my place or filled it full of junk I couldn't stand to look at anymore. No, no. I really liked my little house — the hardwood floors, the dark woodwork, the 1939 Roper stove, the flowering crab out back. But for several years I'd been spending most of my time with a woman who lived across town, and my house had become, in effect, a very expensive studio. When the snow began to melt that year, I felt it was time to sell.

I knew I was going to miss my place in Lakeside, though. Like so many Americans, I'd moved around a lot, always longing for a place I could call my own.

I thought 4621 Jay Street was it. I thought I might live out my days in that small white house with the dark green shutters. But no sooner had my wife and I moved in than our marriage began to fly apart. She was gener-ous enough to leave me the house when we broke up, and I needed it. The house was a haven where I felt free to stare at the wall for hours, reviewing my life like a bad movie. Here I could pace the floors. Here I could sob and shout and kick the furniture. Here I quit drink-ing. Here I quit smoking. Here I made friends with the man in the mirror who had watched me with such con-cern through the years. You develop a lot of affection for a place where that much happens.

I expected preparing my house for the market would be painful, but it really wasn't that bad. I did wonder — when I'd polished the place to a fare-thee-well and brought in plants and put up artwork to impress poten-tial buyers — I did wonder why I was doing all this for strangers when I hadn't managed to do it for myself. But mostly I was proud and glad to be leaving the place in better shape than I'd found it.

I had one painful, strange adventure while cleaning up my house. One day I felt a ghost. I had already made the place about as spiffy as I could, but the day before the realtor was going to start showing the house, I decided to paint the porch — just the front steps and the screen door. They looked a little shabby, and I thought it would be smart to give the buyers a glisten-ing first impression. So I checked an old can in the basement and bought myself a quart of glossy floor and deck enamel. I'm not at all handy, but I knew enough to select a brush with natural bristles for an oil-base paint.

I gathered up tools and materials — screwdriver, hammer, stirring stick, thinner, rags, newspaper — a surprising amount of stuff. I popped the top off the paint can, stirred the rich green paint, dipped my brush, and suddenly missed my grandfather so badly I felt like I'd been stabbed.

It was the smell that did it. I'd been painting inside the house for days with latex and never felt a thing. But the minute I opened that can of old-fashioned oil base, the aroma — pungent as gasoline but sweeter, more mellow — conjured up my grandfather. I thought I knew why. My father had many fine points, but he was useless at home repair. My mother used to save up all such tasks for those rare occasions when her dad would visit. He always brought his toolbox, and he went to work quite cheerfully. He saw fixing stuck drawers, repairing broken handles, painting beat-up tables as both his natural job and hobby. One strong whiff of oil-base paint had brought him back.

My mother and everyone else in her family, including my grandmother, called my grandfather "Pa," so I did, too. Until I was six years old, I thought that was his name. Now as I went to work on the screen door, Pa loomed over me like a genie who'd been released from that can of paint. I saw his white pompadour, his handsome pink Scandinavian face, his impressive belly, the straps of his suspenders. This was a substantial ghost. But then he was gone. Then he was back, smelling of sweat and whiskey and Doublemint gum. Then he was gone. Then he was back. It went on like that all the while I was painting the porch, and I couldn't say which hurt more, Pa's presence or his absence, but it was

sweeter than a dream to be so haunted by a man who
had died twenty-five years back.

Pa called me "Butch," the only nickname I ever had,
and when I was ten, he built me a workbench and gave
me a box of used tools. Was I honored. But Pa lived
hundreds of miles away, I didn't have him around for
encouragement, and the day I gashed myself trying to
make a rubberband gun I pretty much gave up on car-
pentry for good. Was that why Pa had turned up now,
to supervise the final touches I was putting on the
house?

I was down on my knees, slapping paint on the steps
with a bigger brush. Pa was an alcoholic womanizer.
My grandmother left him finally, and he died alone. But
Pa was a good bad man, and his wild example was
important to me. All the men on my father's side were
good good men, gentle and kind but so afraid of the
fire inside they damped it way down and ended up dull,
depressed. So I was especially grateful for this other figure in my background, this big boozy Finn who
chewed snoose and loved to dance the schottische. It
was his kind of trouble I'd chosen in middle age —
women and whiskey — but I'd survived that (barely)
and now I was trying to find a way of life that didn't
depend on the classic choices the older men in my family had made: addiction on the one hand, depression on
the other. Cleaning house and moving out, I'd come to
feel I was leaving the whole first half of my life behind.
It would have been nice to think Pa had showed up to
bless me, but I knew this was only a fantasy generated
by paint fumes.

In any case, the porch was done. I backed away in order to size up my work. The steps and screen door gleamed deep green against the white wall of the house. "Well," I said out loud, "what do you think?" But my grandfather's ghost was gone.

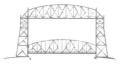

Barber Poles

W hen I moved to Duluth I was determined to economize. I'd chosen a good town in which to be poor. The average house here in the Twin Ports costs about half what it would in the Twin Cities. I wanted to save in smaller ways, too, so I was delighted to see so many barber poles, those medieval symbols that have all but vanished from the streets of sophisticated urban centers.

A barber pole, as any illiterate knows, signifies a barber shop. A barber shop is *not* a hair styling salon. A hair salon is apt to have a clever name (something like "The Upper Cut" or "Hair We Are"), while the name of your average barber shop will demonstrate a distinct lack of imagination ("Second Street Barbers" or "Bob's Barber Shop"). A hair salon will supply loud rock music for your enjoyment or, in a classier joint, something New Age and soothing. Your barber shop, meanwhile, will be silent except for some lazy talk or, possibly, the latest grain prices coming over the radio. The decor of the hair salon will be interesting — maybe lavender and black — and your stylist will be pretty, twenty-seven, and frighteningly friendly. "Hi," she'll say. "I'm Jeanette? I'll be your stylist today?" Your barber shop, on the other hand, will be comfortably nondescript, your barber may well be bald, with a bulge in his middle, and you probably won't learn his name until, on your third visit, you hear another customer call him Warren. Jeanette will show you to a wicker chair, where you'll have to wait, even though you made an appointment. There you can page through the fashion magazines provided by the salon, which exhibit pictures of youngsters with scary hairdos, people who don't look anything like you or anyone you know. Warren will only give you a nod that means: "I'll be with you in a minute. Sit down over there in that straight-back chair and take a look at *Field & Stream*. I don't care if you fish or not." But it's easier and safer to tell these two places apart from the street, before you've entered. A barber shop will have a barber pole. A hair salon will not.

When I lived in Minneapolis I had my hair "styled" for upward of twenty dollars. Plus tip. In Duluth, I discovered I could get my hair "cut" for six bucks. The only difference in the process seemed to be that in the salon the hair person had washed my hair before cutting it, whereas the barber merely dampened my hair a bit, then lowered my ears. I couldn't detect much difference in the end result. Since I normally wash my hair every day anyway, it appeared that in the past I had paid the stylist some fourteen dollars for a redundant shampoo. Plus, of course, the privilege of listening to loud rock music. I was pleased by this discovery, even if it had only come to me in middle age. And I was pleased to be living in Duluth, a city with a dozen barber poles.

But we're not only talking economics here; we're talking sex and myth. I've gone back to the barber shop, at least in part, because the barber shop remains one of the last bastions of male society, and I've decided I want my hair cut by a man. I've been to women stylists who were every bit as skilled as their male counterparts, and maybe more so. The experience of having my hair cut by a woman has been most enjoyable. And that's just the problem. When Jeanette runs her fingers through my hair, I'm apt to grow confused and fall in love, when all I really wanted was a haircut. Maybe I've inherited a little ancient paranoia, too. Remember what happened to Samson when Delilah got her hands on him? Well, I know I'm not about to fall in love with Warren. I feel safe with him.

Maybe what we're talking here, in talking hair and barber shops, is some vestigial form of male initiation rite. Whenever I enter a barber shop, I find myself remembering my father. I recall that once upon a time, when I was very small, barber shops and haircuts made me scared. And it was my father, not my mother, who took me to the barber shop and assured me that this operation wouldn't hurt. And I remember history. If, as a kid, barber poles reminded me of candy canes, I also recall that for hundreds of years barbers were surgeons who bled their customers and pulled their teeth. The red and white stripes of the barber pole really stand for bandages and blood. All this gets confused with cutting hair, which everybody knows is sexual. But no one ever hurt me in a barber shop. I remember my father, the reassuring murmur of male voices, the scent of after-shave and lotions. I remember a grown man, his arms trapped beneath an apron, his neck and face all lathered up, leaning back, while the barber stood beside him with a glinting razor in his hand. I saw, then, that there *are* men who, even when they have you at their mercy, can be trusted not to cut your throat but to touch you with some gentleness and care. That was a good thing to learn back in 1955, and I need to be reminded of it now. Time to get my hair cut.

Existential Baseball

Baseball is a silly sport, the American equivalent of cricket. Hours pass between pitches. Weeks go by between hits. Fat guys stand around, pull up their pants, and spit. Isn't it astonishing that people pay to look at this? I'm a hockey fan myself. Hockey is fast, rough, and graceful. Hockey is primal. Hockey is dangerous. Hockey is clearly a substitute for hunting and war, something you can get yourself worked up about. What's baseball a substitute for? Swinging a stick at a rock? Honestly. The only other sport in which the players spend so much time standing around is highway repair.

Uh-huh. So how come I go down to Wade Stadium so often? Well, for one thing, it's hard to find a good hockey match in July. For another thing, I've got two stepdaughters, and even though baseball bores me, they seem to like it. Or maybe that's not exactly accurate. The girls seem less entertained by the game itself

than by the overall experience of being at the ballpark — watching the crowd and gulping pop and hearing a grown man cry, "Swing, batter batter. Hey, batter
batter." I guess that's what I've come to like, too — not
the game itself so much as the atmosphere. The fragrance of popcorn and cigar smoke on the evening
breeze. The lights and the shouts and the pop of the
ball in the catcher's mitt.

Pro ball came back to Duluth recently . . . even if
only just barely. We're talking quasi-semi-pro ball.
We're talking minor minor league. I'm referring, of
course, to the revival of the highly unlikely Northern
League — dead for twenty-three years — by a bunch of
cross-eyed dreamers. The Northern League must be the
coldest organization in all of professional baseball, seeing that it includes not only the Duluth-Superior Dukes
but the Goldeyes of Winnipeg and the Whiskeyjacks of
Thunder Bay. It's a real possibility for games in this
league to be called on account of snow. These teams
have no affiliation with the major leagues. The players
are paid so poorly they have to room together like college kids. The pitching is wild, the hitting is inexplica-
ble, the fielding frequently looks like some sort of
comedy skit. So far, the Northern League is a smashing
success.

Their first season, Duluth-Superior finished at the
bottom of the league. Then they got worse. But crowds
kept coming to the park anyhow. One reason people
love this brand of ball is that it feels more real than the
major leagues. I went to a Twins game once, years ago,
when they still played at the Met. The stadium was

huge and the players were tiny. The sun shone nice and
bright, Rod Carew got three hits, the Twins won.
Everything was perfect, I guess. I never went back.
I was even less interested once the Twins moved indoors.
But out at Wade Stadium, for less than five bucks, I can
sit so close to the action I'm practically on the field.
And the players are human, too. I couldn't feel a thing
for Kirby Puckett. Puckett was brilliant with a baseball
bat, but his salary was obscene, and his life, at least on
the surface, was nothing but smiles. He might as well
have belonged to a different species. But at Wade
Stadium I can participate in the struggles of my favorite
infielder, who's more like one of us. Let's call him
Mickey Swish. Mr. Swish stands five feet seven inches
short, weighs a scant 165 pounds, and is currently bat-
ting about .175. Mr. Swish is an excellent fielder and
exhibits great enthusiasm for the game, but apparently
he cannot hit the ball. My heart goes out to this man.
I suffer every time he comes to the plate. He loves the
game, he's clearly doomed, he's playing existential baseball — a far scarier sport than what they play in the big
leagues.

Except for his greater competence, courage, and
desire, Mickey Swish reminds me of myself. Back in the
early sixties, back in my early teens, I played second
base — very badly — for the Hanlontown, Iowa, Little
League team. I didn't want to. I already thought baseball was dumb, and it was glaringly apparent that I was
no good at this game. I didn't like the way the ball
stung my hand when I was fortunate enough to catch
it. My fielding was so awful I was always in danger of

getting hit in the face. As a batter I felt lucky when
I grounded out. But Hanlontown was so small that if
I didn't go out for the team, there wouldn't be a team.
My friends begged, and I caved in. As things turned
out, I was the only lousy player on an otherwise memorable team. We had the DeWitt brothers, who could
both hit and run like blazes. We had Dave Haugen,
a violent redhead, who could smack the hide off the ball
and frighten the other team with his freckles and nasty
talk. Mark Jennings pitched a mean curve ball. Halfway
through the season, our coach discovered that Steve
Nannenga — a big, tough, Russian farm kid — could
throw so hard Haugen could hardly hold him. Nannygoat became our secret weapon. He threw so hard he
put dents in the backstop. It didn't hurt at all that he
was wild. Opposing batters barely dared to stand in the
box. We laughed and laughed and beat the pants off
everybody. We beat Kensett. We beat Joice. We even
knocked off Forest City. We won the damn championship, and I've got a flannel patch somewhere that
says so.

My primary contribution to that championship team
was chatter. I loved to smack my glove and make a
racket: "Okay, Nannygoat, come babe, hum babe,
down the old pipe, dust him off, set him down, easy
out." All a batter had to do to shut me up was hit a hot
grounder my way. But I did love to run my mouth. My
only other outstanding contribution to the team was
the high drama I provided at one of our final home
games. We had a small set of bleachers behind home
plate, but most grownups watched the game from their

cars, which were nosed up right close to the field.
They'd honk whenever we got a hit. That night I was
shagging grounders on the sidelines in the pregame
warm-up, concentrating hard, when I ran headfirst into
a car bumper—BONK—and laid myself out flat.
They had to haul me off to the hospital in Mason City,
where a doctor put six stitches in my head.

Given my ridiculous history with baseball, it was
easy for me to get behind a bunch of losers like the
Dukes. I like to be reminded of my own godawful play
and those guys who were so much better than I was—
Nannygoat, Haugen, and the rest. I still think the game
is stupid, but being at the ballpark is a blast. I like to be
reminded of the time I was ten, visiting Duluth, and my
grandpa took me to this very park. I like that Wade
Stadium is out in the working-class part of town, right
next door to the ore docks. I like being so near the lake
that banners of fog drift through the park and the cries
of gulls mingle with those of the crowd. I like the
Dukes' dumb mascot, which looks more like Mister
Peanut than a duke. I like to stand up with my kids and
sing "Take Me Out to the Ball Game" and our team's
theme song, "Duke-Duke-Duke Duke of Earl." I especially enjoy the opportunity to run my mouth again.
I have to exercise restraint, or the kids won't sit with
me, but I still love to growl, "Strike 'im out!" And I'm
glad to know that impulse isn't dying with my genera-
tion. At a recent game I was delighted by a group of
grubby ten-year-olds who refused to go along with the
cheer on the electric scoreboard but instead insisted on
their own:

Existential Baseball

We want a pitcher,
Not a belly-itcher!
We want a pitcher,
Not a belly-itcher!

Music to my ears on a soft summer night at a ballpark
where they play less for pay than out of love and
desperation.

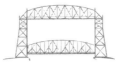

Hawk Ridge

Duluth might lack a professional football team, and sometimes our orchestra squeaks, but the fall hawk migration through this town is undeniably world class. I used to live in Lakeside, a skinny neighborhood at the northeast end of the city, squeezed between Lake Superior and a 400-foot bluff now known as Hawk Ridge. Over thirty years ago, Jack Hofslund, a biologist at the University of Minnesota in Duluth, was working in the yard of his house in Lakeside when he noticed hawks going over and sat down to count. When he got up, hours later, he had tallied ten thousand. Hofslund and others had been keeping track of the fall hawk migration in a casual way for a number of years, but this one day — September 15, 1961 — opened their minds to the magnitude of the phenomenon. Since that time, the Duluth Audubon Society has established a reserve on the hill they dubbed Hawk Ridge, and daily records have been kept each year from summer's end until the stream of raptors peters out in late November. Their highest tally for a single day came to 49,615 hawks on September 18, 1993.

What's behind these huge numbers? A huge body of water. When autumn arrives and the hawks start moving south out of Canada and northern Minnesota, they eventually reach the shore of Lake Superior. Reluctant to cross that inland ocean, the birds drift down the shore, often clustering in swirling groups called "kettles," riding the thermals along the ridgeline, funneling, finally, through the city of Duluth at the south end of the lake, after which the hawks fan out and go their separate ways — some as far as South America.

A dozen different raptors regularly cruise past the Hawk Ridge overlook. They range in size from the bald eagle, with a wingspan in excess of six feet, to the little sharp-shinned hawk, barely bigger than a robin. But size is not a whole lot of help when you're trying to identify raptors at a distance. The experts rely on plumage, shape, and flight. Eagles, for instance, are easy, because when soaring their wings stay straight as boards. The osprey flies with a kind of kink at the elbows, so that it resembles the letter m. A vulture looks like a capital V and always reminds me of a kid's kite because it seems so tippy, so unstable. Some hawks come in both a light phase and a dark, and females might have different plumage from the males, and all the young birds tend to look alike, but when the birds are coming by the dozen you've got to see what's what before they're gone, so sometimes the peaceful job of ornithologist can challenge air traffic control for occupational stress.

For some years now, our official census taker has been Frank Nicoletti, a sturdy, unflappable Italian from upstate New York. As a professional hawk watcher, Frank is a rare bird, but the man loves his work, and he has performed this task for the Fish and Wildlife Service at several spots around the country. Deaf as an infant, Frank only got his hearing after a long series of operations. Because of that early handicap, he says, he's always been especially sharp-eyed, and he began to focus on birds of prey when he was just a boy.

Frank was in high spirits on a recent Friday morning. Tears ran down his cheeks from facing into a cutting wind, but the wind was from the west, and that's the wind that blows the birds out of the woods and down the highways of the sky. A group of amateurs had gathered round to watch and pick up tips. "There's a merlin, folks," Frank said, "coming right at us. Note the pointed wings. Mr. Merlin, speed demon in the world of birds." Now and then Frank spoke into a walkie-talkie to warn the banding station, where the crew employs a pigeon on a harness to lure the predators into nearly invisible nets. "Northern harrier," Frank said. "There's a harrier heading straight down the alley. I hope you guys are listening." Later in the day, Frank would need someone to cover his back while he counted broadwings turning by the hundreds in slow tornadoes over Lake Superior.

To see so many hawks is thrilling, but the real reason I keep stopping at the ridge is the chance for close encounters. Frank has a fake owl stuck on a pole just below the overlook, and when the sharpies skim the treetops they often dart down to check it out. Then they slip along the shoulder of the ridge, seeming close enough to touch. One morning a young bird nearly knocked my cap off. But I keep remembering this roughleg that landed in a dead tree thirty feet in front of me. He held still for several minutes, and I got a good, long look at him. His ivory plumage streaked with brown resembled a warrior's finery. His eye was fierce, alert. His beak looked about as polite as a can opener. His talons meant business, too. While he was resting I kept thinking: wind. If wind had a body it would be this bird. And then he lifted off.

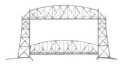

The Cider Man

Paul Steklenski is the cider man of Duluth. A tall fellow with a brindled beard, Paul reminds me of a sheepdog. He seems both shy and friendly. Well into his forties now, he only just got married a couple of years ago. I think of Paul as the last of the red-hot hippies. By which I mean, money doesn't run him. By which I mean, this man wants to give instead of grab. His life, in fact, seems organized around the act of feeding others. He works at the Positively Third Street Bakery. And every fall he gives his neighbors cider by the gallon.

About ten years ago, when Paul was working in the local food co-op, they got a shipment of cider from Bayfield, Wisconsin, that impressed him so much he offered a sample to a friend. "No thanks," she said. "We press our own." And Paul was hooked. He started helping out his friends, and soon he bought equipment of his own. Later he replaced that with some better gear that he had custom-built. His stainless steel chopper was made in a local machine shop. Paul built the wooden parts of his cider press himself, but the heavy metal screw — a real thing of beauty — came off an antique printing press his brother found out East. Today, with a little help and this simple equipment, Paul can turn out fifty gallons of cider in an hour.

I'm not sure how his pressing parties come to pass. Paul sends out a couple postcards, makes a few phone calls. People gossip, and word gets around. I showed up early one year, with two bushels of Haralsons I'd picked off our tree, teetering on a creaky stepladder, my face in cool dry leaves. Other folks appeared before long with boxes, bags, and baskets of their own. Not to worry. Our host already had plenty of fruit stacked up around the chopper. Paul is an apple outlaw, with many secret sources. He picks all through the fall, keeping his eye out for vacant lots with forgotten trees and abandoned farms with orchards going wild. He'll pick a hundred bushels in a season, himself, so there's always a strong supply.

Everyone found a job, somebody switched on the chopper, and we were under way. A couple of adults took charge of dumping apples in the chopper tray, snatching out the bad ones, making sure we got a mix of sweet and tart varieties. Teenagers stood by with sticks, controlling the flow, clearing out the jam-ups. Somebody changed buckets underneath the chopper and hauled the mash to the press, where we dumped it into a big nylon bag, which we dropped inside a wooden cage. The mash was so heavy it pressed itself; juice ran through the slats of the cage as soon as the bag hit the boards. Somebody moaned. Somebody whooped. My partner dropped the lid on the cage, and I spun the wheel that lowered the screw that squeezed the juice from the apple mash. Cider ran into the buckets like rain. Somebody grabbed a glass and we sampled the stuff. Praise God from whom all blessings flow, the cider was good again this year — tangy and sweet, full-bodied and strong, rich as home-brewed beer.

After half an hour, I took a break and looked around at my neighbors dumping apples in the chopper tray, at a woman using a baseball bat to tighten the screw on the cider press, at a boy wheeling a barrow full of apple pulp down the hill to Paul's garden plot. My hands were sticky with apple juice, my clothes were spattered with apple flesh. A man and his daughter were funneling cider into a long line of jugs. Near the wall of the house, a young woman jerked up her shirt and gave her infant suck. In the midst of it all stood the cider man, listening to a friend, his arms crossed, his knees bent, leaning back, laughing at the sky. My God, I thought, this is erotic, this is medieval, this looks like one of those pictures by Brueghel.

We were done for the day in an hour, and we went our separate ways, our jugs of liquid gold in hand. But Paul would go on pressing through October, putting on a show for the YMCA, giving the Cub Scouts something fun to do, calling other people in for parties.

Back home, I poured myself a short glass of cider and put the jugs out on the porch where they would keep cool. I raised my glass in a solitary toast to the passing season. Half the leaves were already down. What leaves were left were brilliant, the sky was bright, and I was glad. There was trouble overseas, there was murder in

Minneapolis, terrible things were happening right close
to home, but I was happy because Paul Steklenski had
invented an autumn ritual that helped hold our neighborhood together, a ritual that built community and
deepened all our lives. What generosity, I thought. And
where was his reward?

I thought I knew. I remembered Paul's laughter as he
watched the proceedings at the cider press. And I
remembered how, halfway through the pressing, we'd
run short of apples. Paul had led us then into his basement, where he'd laid up his supply. There were boxes
by the dozen. The fruit was piled high. What hit me,
though, wasn't the number of apples so much as their
scent. The air in there was so mysterious and sweet you
could get inebriated just by breathing in and out.
I thought about that fragrance now as I sipped the last
of my drink. I thought how that fruity incense must
permeate Paul's house, and how the nights were getting cold and longer now, and how, night after night,
all through the fall, the cider man and his wife would
be drifting off to sleep to the sweet perfume of apples.

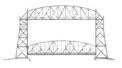

The Season of Death

Autumn is the season that Duluth does best. Winters are fierce and linger too long. If you leave town for so much as a single weekend in May, you risk missing spring altogether. Summers can be splendid, but some are entirely illusory, lost in the fog and drizzle. Come September, though, the sky often clears, and the landscape lights up so ferociously that you moan with amazement.

This blazing, bittersweet season normally lasts at least two months — from Labor Day, say, to Halloween. We're just about done with this year's edition. Already we've watched the maple leaves flare and fall. Over the hill, the woods have gone gray except for the glow of the tamaracks. Down in Duluth and along the North Shore, the oak leaves still shimmer as if they were cut out of copper, and the leaves of the popples gleam like gold coins; but we know what's coming. Already we've seen the scarlet crab apples frosted with snow. We've heard the geese going south in the night. And the silver salmon, driven by their own kind of homesickness and sexual desperation, have thrashed up the narrow tributaries of Lake Superior to spawn in shallow pools, where they weaken, tarnish, darken, and die.

This is the season of death. The signs are everywhere. The scent of woodsmoke is its perfume and so is the aroma of exhausted leaves. I wonder why, when I'm moving right along through middle age, why don't I mind being reminded of my mortality every which way I look? Time is obviously running out, and I'm haunted by what I've lost, by all that I've failed to accomplish. After all these years, I still don't have a respectable job, or a pension plan, or health insurance. I ought to be depressed, and I am, but still I walk the streets of my neighborhood, kicking the leaves, up to my ankles in nature's confetti, feeling half crazy with happiness. The dead leaves resemble the garish currency of some small foreign country, and I've actually caught myself thinking, *This* is my money!

What's wrong with me? I ought to be sunk in gloom, whining about the onset of winter, but instead I want to quote poetry, and I do. These lines by John Engman, for instance:

> Am I poor?
> Are the leaves falling because I can't afford them?
> Am I crazy? I think the leaves are falling because
>   I can't afford them.
> Am I alone? Autumn leaves are falling like little
>   lessons

but I haven't learned anything.
The wind is cold and the leaves have fallen for
   three days.

Or the wonderful, simple conclusion to Rilke's
"October Day":

Whoever has no house by now will not build.
Whoever is alone now will remain alone,
will wait up, read, write long letters,
and walk along sidewalks under large trees,
not going home, as the leaves fall and blow away.

Why don't these words discourage me? How come the
sadness of this season makes me glad?
   I have to conclude that even as the dying leaves
enrich the soil, awareness of my own mortality nour-
ishes my life. Some secret part of me is downright
delighted that I'm going to die. That secret self is bored
by the notion of eternal life and understands that nothing would be solved by living on and on. The fantasy of
everlasting life is apt to put me to sleep, but every
autumn I feel energized, awakened. Reminded that my
time is limited, I pay more attention to the passing
moment. My pulse quickens, and I notice that the fallen
birch leaves aren't just yellow but a dozen different
shades, and this year's apple cider tastes especially
sweet.
   This morning I'm convinced that it's my job as I
grow older to fall more and more in love with life while
growing less and less afraid of death. I'm grateful to my
own dear dead who have taught me this. I thank my
mother, whose voice has faded to a whisper now, whose

face I can't recall without the help of photographs. I thank my good friend Joe, who years ago went down to the river on a lovely autumn day and shot himself. I thank my old lover Arlinda, who was bald at the end, thanks to the chemotherapy, but who held me with a steady gaze, her clear eyes crackling with honesty and challenges. I say thanks again to my grandmother, who lived to be ninety-seven, raucous with laughter to the last. These dead people — these memories — are my teachers. Thanks to them, my life seems a gift, and death feels far less frightening than it did when I was young. These are my good ghosts, and they come especially close in late October as we celebrate All Souls', "as the leaves fall and blow away."

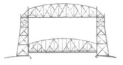

Disorganized Hockey

It's hockey season in Duluth. All over town, day and night, you hear the scrape of skate blades and the thwack of pucks being banged off the boards of neighborhood rinks. When I walk to the corner store, I stop to watch the kids practicing at the outdoor rink. The coach and his assistant bark out commands, encouragement, and reprimands to the boys going through their drills. I don't know what they call this program — Midgets, Mites, Peewees, Piss-ants? — but these boys are awfully small. They seem overburdened by the weight of their equipment. I'm touched by the earnestness and effort with which they strain to master skills still beyond their little bodies. I love to watch them practice, but it all seems terribly serious.

Don't get me wrong. I am not one of those cranks who believe competitive athletics promote hostility in our society. I participated in competitive sports myself back in high school; I enjoyed myself and learned a lot.

Mostly what I learned was how to lose, and because, as adults, what we mostly do is lose — parents, lovers, jobs, our fondest dreams — that was invaluable training. I was best at football, a game in which determination can compensate for lack of talent. I loved that rough-neck sport. Here in middle age, however, I realize I've not only forgotten the scores of all the games in which I played, I've also lost most of my memories of daily practice. Today, I couldn't care less about football. I never play touch, never go to games at any level. I suspect that my participation in an organized program wore out my enthusiasm.

Yet hockey, which I never played with any serious-ness, still has a hold on me. My memories of that sport are all disorganized, but the first and most powerful still glows for me like red-hot iron. Until the age of six, I lived outside of Roseau in the tiny town of Ross, a hamlet so small it hardly deserved a name. Ross was a creamery, a post office, a general store, a grade school, and a hockey rink. One cold night when I was five my mother took me to the rink to skate beneath the flood-lights. A few farmboys had driven into town to knock a puck around, and in the darkness of the warming house, which smelled of wool and woodsmoke, they offered to burn my name into the handle of my sawed-off hockey stick. I was afraid of those giants, so I looked to my mother. She must have agreed, because one of those teenagers pulled a red-hot poker from the flaming mouth of the barrel stove and branded the handle of my hockey stick with my first name. Still today, this instant, I can see that magic word appear and breathe an incense more exotic than the smell of sandalwood.

What was it I felt when that teenager handed back my stick with a man's rough laugh? Proud, scared, accepted, a little wounded, somehow, as if he'd branded me instead of my stick. I was a boy. I would be big. I would be like him. That was a primal experience, and the memory of it warms me on many winter nights.

When my family moved away to southern Minnesota, one of those farmboys, Maynard Braaten, warned me that down on the Iowa border I'd have to skate on a cow pie. Well, it was true the school had no hockey program. But there was the river, and sometimes we were lucky: the river froze up nice and hard before the snow arrived. Then the neighbor boys and I would skate for miles up the river, speeding over clear, black ice, passing a puck as we went. Now and then we'd pause to investigate a beaver den or munch a snack. Sometimes we had to slow for botchy ice or open water, but usually, as I remember, we flew. When the snow piled up, we struggled to maintain an open space for river hockey, but the work was worth the effort, especially on those Sunday afternoons when our fathers honored us by joining in. Once even our mothers came, with white figure skates and baskets packed with food. We built a crackling fire right there on the river, creating a kind of chaotic community picnic in the snow. Every Christmas until recently, when my father grew too frail, my family held to this tradition with a hockey free-for-all. We'd clear a space on a local pond, and then girls and women, boys and men, some in skates and some in sloppy overshoes, with shovels, brooms, and one or two cracked hockey sticks, with whoops and shouts and giggling fits, we'd whack away at a puck for an hour, which was far more fun than opening our presents.

Given my history with hockey as a friendly form of anarchy, I can't say I envy those little squirts I see practicing so hard at local rinks. They've got gear, coaches, schedules, cheering crowds, and a dandy sheet of ice. But I had ponds and rivers, and when I imagine what these tiny guys are likely to remember when they reach my age, I'm sure I wouldn't trade my memories for theirs. With hockey I was lucky, and from here on out, I want all my sports slaphappy and disorganized.

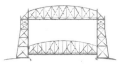

The History of Snow

It's not unusual for winter to arrive in Duluth well before Thanksgiving. A couple years back, we got socked with seven inches of snow just a few days after Halloween. First a fierce wind came howling down Lake Superior, working the water into eight-foot breakers that smashed the piers and seawalls. Then we got a hard rain that turned to snow and fell all through the night. The flakes were still flying the following morning, when I found myself stuck in an extended argument with my know-it-all stepdaughter.

I had casually referred to the weather we were having as a blizzard. She, who had recently entered a highly contrary stage of life, insisted this was only a snowstorm. Normally, I tried to let such insignificant contradictions pass, figuring she was only exerting her preadolescent sense of independence. But wild weather excites me, and I was not about to let her undercut my exhilaration with a smarty-pants remark like that. I'm

not sure what the difference between a blizzard and
a snowstorm is, if there is any, but having suffered
through forty-odd winters I think I by God know
a blizzard when I see one. So for several minutes, the
girl and I were warmly engaged in a "'tis," "'tisn't,"
"snowstorm," "blizzard" argument. At last I was moved
to make a twenty-five-cent wager, which my opponent
accepted with a hot handclasp. But then we realized we
would need an arbiter. I suggested the radio DJ of her
choice. "If he calls this a blizzard, or if there are any
school closings whatsoever — even one — you're done,
I'm right, you're wrong, and you owe me a quarter." She
agreed to these terms and stomped off to her room,
where the radio was permanently tuned to one of those
obnoxious stations teenagers enjoy. Inside five minutes
she was back, offering me a shiny new quarter and
a series of properly respectful bows. I found the first
snowfall of that season particularly pleasing.

But actually venturing out in all that weather was
a shock. First I had to dig out boots and gloves and the
soft black cap with earflaps that embarrasses my family.
And then to clear the sidewalk, shovel out the cars, and
scrape the damn windshields, getting snow down my
neck and up my sleeves — it all seemed so much trouble. The snow had come so early! And was bound to
last so long! I've always been a proud cold-weather
man, but more and more as I go on, I understand those
people in their sixties who flee for Texas with the first
stiff breeze.

Once upon a time it wasn't so. The first snowfall that
I recall was like a miracle. I must have been four years
old. We lived north of Roseau then, just south of the

Canadian border. I was playing in the backyard,
I remember, when feathers started falling out of the sky.
Stunned with wonder, I stopped what I was doing and
caught some fluff on my cowboy glove. I'd heard about
this. This was snow. I went up to the front yard to see if
it was snowing there, too. Yup. Snow was happening all
over, falling fast from a dark gray sky. My dad had
made a hut for me in the backyard by nailing some
weathered boards between two trees and tacking a roof
on top. I retreated to my hut for shelter now and
crouched there on my haunches, out of the wind,
watching the snow drift up in little waves against the
green grass. I thought the snow looked like my mom's
laundry detergent, but it tasted okay, not at all like
soap. I remember squatting there in my hut a long time,
looking out at the snow. I remember the tail of my
coonskin cap brushing my cheek and the cold, new
smell of the snow. Yellow lights came on inside the
house, and my mother called my name, but I didn't
answer. I was too pleased to be right where I was,
pleased by the privacy of my little house, amazed to
watch the sky fall down and down and cover all the
ground with white.

One snow sets off another in my mind, and I remember forts and igloos I constructed with my pals; the
warm, safe sensation of drowsing in the car while my
father drove us through a blizzard, snowflakes swarm-
ing through the headlights like electric glowworms;
once when we got stuck in a flat, plain world of white,
and my father had to hike away into the night to call a
tow truck; another time, when we were out alone, just
the two of us, and my father stopped the car in the

middle of the snow-packed gravel road, making me get out and come around and look up where he pointed in that tree right there, and there it was — a bobcat! — and I stared — glad, thrilled, scared — as the snow fell softly all around us.

Such memories constitute the history of snow as I know it, a history I need to read again each year as we approach the winter solstice. Otherwise, I'm apt to hate the stuff, to see it as a seasonal annoyance, something to be gotten through. That's a pretty stupid attitude to cling to when you live in northern Minnesota, where the ground is sometimes white for half a year. Back in my bitter drinking days, I used to entertain an even dumber notion: that winter was a punishment God had dreamed up just for me. But snow, up here at least, is simply how things are. Reality. Love it or leave it. Myself, I aim to stay.

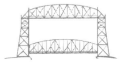

Hibernation

Here in middle age, I've learned to be a boy again, to welcome the initial blizzard of the season. Recently we got a doozy, with big winds sweeping down the lake and lightning flashing through clouds of snow. How strange to hear thunderclaps in a snowstorm. But that seemed appropriate, too — like a declaration of winter. I wouldn't have been surprised to hear opera — "The Ride of the Valkyries" — coming out of those storm clouds. Next morning school was called off, and most everyone stayed home from work. We got out the goose down, the thick, leather mitts, the mukluks and Sorels. We dug out the cars and hollered greetings to our neighbors. Oddly enough, I didn't hear one complaint about the weather all the livelong day.

I'm not complaining now, either. After the lush greenery of summer and the spectacular colors of fall, I'm excited about hibernation. I'm tired of my own busyness. "The world is too much with us," wrote

William Wordsworth two hundred years back. "Getting and spending we lay waste our powers." Wordsworth didn't know the half of it. He didn't have TV news and frozen cars and jangling phones to ruin his day. I've got two jobs and write on the side. My wife has a job and a mini-business after hours. On the weekends we do laundry and pick up the house. In between times there's dinner and dishes and driving the kids to piano and parties, the ski hill and scouts. *Did anyone feed the chinchilla? Who's taking the dog to the vet? Would someone please answer the phone?* So it goes, day after day. And so I say, bring on the blizzards and subzero temps.

One of the great consolations of the vicious winter weather we get up here in northern Minnesota is that everyone has to slow down. From December through March, all plans become provisional. I've often thought we ought to cancel January altogether, everybody just stay home and eat up the leftover Christmas cookies. It's plainly crazy to expect cars to start and hum along happily at twenty below. It's nuts to think people will come to work when the sky has dumped a half foot of snow. Why should we keep trying to live according to clocks and schedules when the world is frozen solid? Animals have more sense than that. They hole up, hide out, and shut down.

Once I had the good luck to observe a hibernating bear. My buddy Dexter guided me to the bear den, which his brother had discovered near his cabin in the woods. It was a gray day, and the woods were cold and bare. After five minutes of crunching through the snow, we were completely surrounded by naked, look-alike trees, and I had no idea where we were.

"I hope you know where you're going," I said to Dexter's back. "I wouldn't have the foggiest how to find my way out of here."

Dexter turned and gave me a look that was part pity, part wonder, but mostly disgust. "You might try following the trail we've been stomping into the snow."

"Oh," I said. "Sorry."

Another five minutes, and we came right up on the rim of the den. "There," Dexter said, pointing.

"Where?"

"Right there, for godsake. Don't step on him."

The den was nothing but a hole in the ground, and we were standing on the edge. The bear looked like a heavy rug with leaves and twigs and bits of bark scattered over it. I saw the black fur rise and fall as the bear breathed, and then I made out the head.

"Amazing," I said. "How cool!"

Dexter chuckled with satisfaction, and we stood there chatting happily until the bear must have heard us in his sleep because he turned his head and snapped at us. *Clack-clack-clack.* A disturbing sound. We backed away, deciding we'd seen enough. But ever since that day, I've thought getting fat in the fall and sleeping most of the winter might not be a bad idea. That bear looked damn cozy.

Human beings aren't half as wise, but at least we're allowed to slow down once the Christmas frenzy has passed. Usually we get a few days, anyhow, when the temperatures drop so low the cars refuse to start or blizzards simply fill the streets. There's no going anywhere then, and we're able to enjoy the human form of hibernation at last. We stoke up the stove and put on the coffee. We pair off for Scrabble or haul out a puzzle with a thousand bewildering pieces. After a while, our girls might even resort to the dollhouse they haven't touched in years. My wife will fire up the sewing machine or dig out her box of pastels. Maybe I'll snow-shoe up to the video store for a movie. Maybe the neighbors will wallow over for cocoa. Maybe I'll shovel the walk . . . maybe not. No, I think I'll take a little nap.

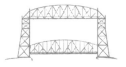

Jangle Bells

'Tis the season, as psychologists keep warning us, of depression and of suicide. You know the reasons: four o'clock sunsets and ten below, financial fidgets and shopping fatigue, competitive gift-giving, competitive gift-making, competitive gift-wrapping, cookie bloat. Christmas is a killer. But I've survived dozens of these unholy holidays, and if your nerves are jangled by Salvation Army bells, if Christmas carols sound down-right funereal to you, I have a few suggestions.

The first may seem a bit extreme, but, believe me, this one works. Leave the country. I once had the great good luck to pass a Christmas in Paris. It barely touched me. On Christmas Eve my wife and I watched the sophisticated French make fools of themselves as they fought each other for admission to the mass at Notre Dame. The next day in our cheap hotel room we made Christmas dinner out of olives, bread, paté, and a bottle of dark red wine. We didn't have a relative

within a thousand miles. That was a completely pain-
less Christmas.

Suggestion number two. Ignore it. Notify your
friends and relatives that you're not celebrating this
year. Let them know ahead of time you don't want any
presents and warn them that they won't be getting
any either. They'll be upset, but so what? The holidays
make most adults unhappy anyway, and you'll save
both grief and money. It may be difficult pretending
Christmas isn't there with all those carols in the air,
but you can do it. Use a little ingenuity. I spent one
Christmas hiding in a movie house. When I finally
emerged from the theater I was slightly cross-eyed,
but the whole blessed holiday was over.

If you have kids, you'll be too broke to leave the
country, and you'll have to celebrate. But for pity's sake,
remember: no law says you have to haul the little nip-
pers to your parents' place. Think a minute. Do you
really need to see your parents *now*? You know what's
going to happen. Even though you're bald or gray,
you'll turn into a sulky teenager the moment you walk
in the door. For Adult Children of Parents, any
encounter with the folks is bound to provoke a certain
amount of pain. So why not save your visit for some
holiday that's easier — like Easter?

Even minor violations of tradition will tend to ease
your stress. Wrap your gifts in newspaper, like fish. Just
slap it on with tape. Two days after Christmas hardly
anyone remembers what they got from whom, let alone
how all those things were wrapped. If you're weary of
pretending you like lutefisk and lefse, give it up, at least
this once. Drag the Weber out of the garage and grill

some T-bones in the snow. Your kids will be delighted by such foolishness, and you'll all be glad to be reminded summer's on the way.

Which, after all, is what this holiday is all about. Or was, before the businessmen and Christians got ahold of it. Long before the glitzy merchandisers came to town, long before Bishop Liberius of Rome stole the winter solstice for the birthday of Christ, people celebrated the birthday of the sun. Keep this in mind, and you'll be able to forgive yourself if you've been feeling bad. It's *natural* to be depressed this time of year. The primal, raw reality is that the days have been shrinking for six months as if the world were coming to an end. But on December 22 that will change. Why not celebrate the pagan holiday on which the Christian and commercial ones are based? The example of Christ may only deepen your depression as you compare His perfect love to your own grumpy attitude. The economy may be in the dumpster and your checkbook full of blanks. But here in Minnesota, anyhow, we've still got plenty of wood. Build a bonfire, gather round, and as the sparks fly out of sight help the sun come back to life by chanting Goethe's deathbed words: "More light! More light!"

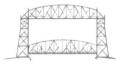

A Christmas Card

Of all the peculiar pleasures of the winter holidays, the habit of exchanging Christmas cards seems especially bittersweet and strange. This custom may be more meaningful than nibbling fruitcake, but it's a lot less fun than hauling a tree inside the house. I often wonder why we bother. My heart is hardly gladdened when I receive a prefab greeting graced by nothing but the signature of somebody I used to know. All I get from such a gift is a sad little vision of my name scratched off a list. It helps if the sender has scrawled a personal note, but what can anybody say in such a small space? The message all these cards deliver is essentially the same: "Hi there. Even though we never get together anymore, I still think about you now and then." What a melancholy custom! It really deserves detailed analysis by some smart young anthropologist. The sorrow and the pity of ritualistic Christmas card exchange is immediately apparent when you consider what we actually do with the cards. At most, we tape them to a door frame or collect them in a basket and then sometime in February maybe give them one last glance before we throw them out.

Christmas cards are highly disposable items. I confess I've grown so jaded that I often open them over the trash and let them drop as soon as I've studied the signatures. So it seems somewhat surprising that my grandmother preserved one Christmas card for sixty years and passed it on to me before she died. I'm even more surprised to find I count this Christmas card as one of my most prized possessions.

My Grandma Eastman spent her later years in a Minneapolis high-rise but lived most of her life in Duluth. I stopped for coffee at her tiny high-rise apartment fairly often, and, especially after I had moved up north, I pestered her for stories about the old days in Duluth. Gram had a fine appreciation for quirky characters, and one afternoon she got to talking about "that Swedish painter we used to know." When I pressed her, she remembered that his name was Heldner . . . Knute Heldner. By this time I knew that Knute Heldner was about the only noteworthy artist Duluth had ever produced, and I was flabbergasted that my grandparents, who were distinctly working class, had actually known him. But Gram not only had all kinds of details on the man — he'd bought a used car from my grandparents, his wife had a French name, they lived in a loft downtown, he was shy and wild but liked my grandmother's pumpernickel bread — not only that, but she polished off her story by producing concrete proof. "He sent us a handmade Christmas card from Paris," Gram said. "I've got it tucked away, back there in my cedar chest."

Today, I keep the card and its envelope between two pieces of acid-free mat board, wrapped in all-rag tissue paper. Some day, when I can afford it, I'll have the card and envelope framed side-by-side. Both have turned light brown with age; both are slightly brittle. The ink on the envelope looks chocolate rather than black or blue, and the handwriting is baroque with flourishes, a relic from the days when penmanship was not only a course in school but a matter of personal pride. The upper right corner of the envelope is missing; no doubt my grandmother clipped the exotic stamp and gave it to some young collector.

The card itself is a five-by-seven-inch sheet on top of which is glued a smaller three-by-five. Pressed into the smaller sheet is a woodblock print of Mary and her infant son, who are being visited by some shepherds and their sheep. The draftsmanship is less than brilliant. The baby Jesus looks more like a two-year-old than a newborn; he seems sort of muscle-bound, and he's got a thick, black shock of hair. The shepherds appear to have tonsured haircuts, so they resemble monks. One of the sheep could easily be taken for a dog; the other looks like a small cow. The third man in the picture might be Joseph; or he might be a wise man offering some sort of incense; or he could be a servant holding a bowl of steaming porridge. It's just not entirely clear. But the composition is very pleasing, and the picture has a lovely, silvery look, as if it had been done with ink and soft gray pencil. The print has been signed in a small, sharp hand; and underneath the print, Matthew 7, verse 12, has been written in French. In English, that passage reads, "Therefore all things whatsoever ye would that men should do to you, do ye even so to them: for this is the law and the prophets." The back of the card is signed, "Joyeux Noël, From Knute and Colette Heldner, Paris 1929."

This fragile Christmas card is my family's one, thin, tenuous but genuine connection to the glamorous world of Paris in the twenties. It also serves me as a kind of totem, a reminder that authentic art can be produced even in places as provincial as Duluth. For Knute Heldner returned from Europe in 1932 and made many fine paintings here over the next twenty years, winning acclaim in places as far away as Chicago, New Orleans, Stockholm, and Paris. Contemporary painters, writers, and composers hard at work in the heartland can take encouragement from Heldner's example. I sure do. And I like remembering that immigrant artist's kindness in sending a hand-fashioned Christmas card to my grandparents, lo, those many years ago. Heldner could not have known that his small act of generosity would also be a kindness unto me, two generations later. But so it was, and so it is. And so I have been moved at last to write this rather lengthy and belated Christmas card to a minor Swedish-American artist, dead for forty-four years, in a futile but sincere attempt to return one kindness for another. "For this is the law and the prophets."

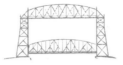

Afterthoughts on Christmas Trees

Normally, a week or two into the new year, we plant our Christmas tree in a snowdrift with some suet for the birds dangling from the branches. This year, though, we took our tree to a recycle site where city workers ran it through a chipper. I like to think our tree, which served so well as a symbol of renewal, might have a practical afterlife. In Duluth, I'm told, the chipped-up trees are used as mulch on hiking trails. I hope that's true, because we sure go through a passel of trees. If this is a city of a hundred thousand, and you figure we average four people per household, that means we sacrifice twenty-five thousand trees every Christmas.

Don't get excited. I'm not about to propose that we abolish the grand old tradition of putting up a tree at Christmas. It's just that here in the blessed calm following the holidays, I've been struck by the dimensions of the Christmas tree phenomenon. I mean, if you figure one tree for an average household of four, we must have

killed a million evergreens in Minnesota last month.
I hate to think about the country as a whole. Let's see.
Two hundred fifty million divided by four . . . comes
to . . . more than sixty million trees? Can that be? No,
I'd better divide that sum by half to account for Jews,
Muslims, Buddhists, and others who may not participate in this odd annual ritual. Thirty million is still a
staggering figure. It's interesting to see how we can get
worked up about the rain forests on another continent
but don't mind wasting millions of our conifers just to
celebrate a passing holiday.

But as I say, I'm not opposed to this peculiar custom.
Just the opposite, in fact. I'm growing more devoted to
it as I go along. There were winters in my twenties
when I did without a tree, for sure, but that was less
from principle than laziness. Besides, I could always
count on older friends and relatives to carry on the tradition. I'll bet if everyone had gone without a tree in
those days, I would have been seriously upset. At any
rate, here in middle age, the darkness of the winter
months seems awfully deep to me, suggesting, I suppose, that final, utter darkness that comes closer
every day. So I appreciate those old symbols of
renewal — lights and greenery — a little more each
year. The straight white spruce that stood in our back
room this season, laden with tinsel and silly decorations, looked strangely brave to me. And I'm grateful,
here in January, to see the odd wreath hanging on a
neighbor's door and colored lights still twinkling on the
trees and snow-caked houses. Did I once think that
such displays were vulgar, dumb, and wasteful? I'm
afraid I did. Now they seem cheerful and tragic. It's a

cold planet, baby, and we come to a cold end. Trees
and lights both help along the way.

But the idea of bringing a tree inside the house! You
know, it's damn near as weird as if you'd suddenly
decided to keep a cow in the living room. "There, now,
Bessie. Stay." You give the tree a drink of water, too,
now and then, don't you? This can't be a Christian idea.
Of course it's not. The Christians would like you to
think so . . . stick a pretty angel on the treetop and pre-
tend. But the habit of putting up a tree at Christmas
time has much deeper roots. We know, for example,
that the Romans traded greenery on the first of January.
Celtic druids, the priests of ancient Ireland, believed
that oak trees and mistletoe were sacred. My encyclopedia, speculating about the origin of Christmas trees,
says straight out: "People in Scandinavia once wor-
shiped trees." The primal truth is this: When we cut a
living tree on one of the darkest days of the year, stand
it up inside the home, and dress it with decorations, we
are performing a pagan sacrifice to make the sun come
back. When we sink a sawblade into the slender trunk
of a young fir tree, we draw sap instead of blood, but in
that moment we are one with the ancient people — pic-
tured in the Bible, Homer's epic poems, and many other
places — who cut the throats of oxen, sheep, and goats
to offer up on altars.

Of course if you just buy your tree precut from a
commercial lot, you're not apt to be reminded of blood
sacrifice. But up here in northern Minnesota, there's
plenty of opportunity to cut your own, and when I saw
my dad during the holidays this year, I thought once
more of the very first Christmas I can recall and the

first Christmas tree I ever saw cut. I was four or five then, and those were the days when my father had black, wavy hair and strong arms. Today he is frail and unsteady, with dry, wispy hair, and glasses that slide down his nose. These days, my father forgets. More and more often he seems to be lost in some sort of internal blizzard, and as his memories gradually fade, I feel compelled to remember aloud for us both. That particular Christmas, I remember, the Nordvalls had invited us to take a tree from their woods. So my dad drove out to their place on Minnesota Hill and hauled me along. The Nordvall place was a subsistence dairy farm, located on the only high ground in that flat country, backed up against the Canadian border — a wild, hardscrabble, pioneer farm at the end of the road. The snow lay so deep that I had to ride my father's shoulders as he plowed across the pasture to the forest. The woods were full of shadows, and I was scared that we'd get lost in there or something bad would get me, but we didn't have to go in very far. My father chose a dark green tree that seemed extremely tall to me, and he made me stand back farther than I wanted. Never very practical or handy, he had brought a carpenter's crosscut saw, but it seemed to work all right. I can still hear it gnawing at the trunk and see the yellow sawdust spurt out in the snow and hear my father cry, "Timberrr!" The tree tipped and fell with a rush and snow flew off in all directions. In the soft silence afterward, a chickadee sang somewhere. My father hoisted the tree up on his shoulder, and I wallowed along behind, up toward the red sheds and the house with sweet smoke curling from the chimney and the woodpile high as the house.

Inside, there was laughter and old people with white
hair who spoke Swedish and gave me sheets of brittle
flatbread and a mug of hot milk.

I'm not so much for New Year's resolutions anymore,
but I remember that scene from my boyhood, way back
there when my father was a giant, and I remember what
my encyclopedia told me, that my ancestors once wor-
shiped trees, and I resolve that this coming Christmas
I will go into the woods to cut my own green tree.

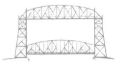

Finlandia at Fourteen Below

It's deep winter now, and I am playing *Finlandia*. I still make mistakes, but the music is recognizable, and this is a minor miracle because four months ago I couldn't play the piano at all. I have labored at this piece like an athlete, day after day for weeks, and I've just about got it at last. Sometimes my fingers remember the way, and we march through both pages without one wrong note. To master a piece of music, I'm learning, you have to absorb it into your body. Fourteen below. This room is cold, but *Finlandia* warms my bones.

I always liked music. I sang alongside my dad in church choir when I was a kid, I took chorus in high school, I even sang in a couple of specialty groups, like boys' quartet. But that was way back in the Pleistocene, and the truth is I never knew what I was doing. My technique consisted of standing beside Jim DeWitt, a guy with a booming bass voice who could read music, and trying to match the sounds that issued from his mouth. The actual system of musical notation — lines and squiggles, black spots and flags — that language looked more foreign to me than Icelandic. Besides, it was already clear that my brother was going to be the true musician in our family. Besides that, my step-mother played the piano quite well, and I wasn't about to put myself in a position where I'd have to ask her for help. There were just too many other interesting things to do: reading and writing and sports and hiking off in the woods and mooning around about girls. So for years and years I was content to let music remain a mystery.

But I always liked to listen, and one summer in my early teens, when I stayed for a couple of weeks with an older cousin, I went way beyond rock 'n' roll. My cousin had started a classical record collection, and he urged me to sample this music when he was off working his job as a lifeguard. Alone in that house above the Mississippi River, I heard for the first time the extra-ordinary sounds of Beethoven's Fifth Symphony, Tchaikovsky's 1812 Overture, and other glorious musi-cal contraptions that seem specifically designed to cap-ture the souls of teenage boys. Among the many wonders in my cousin's collection was an album by the Mormon Tabernacle Choir, and among the several works included on that album, the one that moved me most was something called *Finlandia* by Jan Sibelius.

Finlandia quickened my heart and stirred the hair on the back of my neck. *Finlandia* made me both happy and sad. *Finlandia* made me proud of my Scandinavian ancestors. "On great lone hills," the lyrics began, in the version sung by the Tabernacle Choir, *"on great lone hills, where tempests brood and gather."* For a melancholy teenager, this was perfect poetry, and even today, when I sit down and strike those first four chords — *bahm, bahm, bahm, bahm* — I see Nordic landscape. I'm noticing notes, of course, but I'm also looking right through the page, right through the piano, at snow sweeping down through the valley and evergreens mounting the ridge-line and a last burst of sunshine that breaks through the gathering gloom.

Finlandia is stately and grand. I can slump when I work on the blues, but *Finlandia* demands that I sit up straight. That summer in my cousin's house when I first heard it, the music drew me to my feet. So when I say *Finlandia* moved me, I don't merely mean I was touched, though it's true the music made me crazy with feelings of triumph and sorrow and dozens of other emotions for which we have no names. But when I say this music moved me, I mean *Finlandia* made me stand before the picture window to dip and bow and shake my head and thrash my arms as though I were conducting, as though the natural world outside that window needed my instructions or assent, as though the trees that swayed in the summer breeze needed me to lead them, to tell them, yes! be trees! be green! as though the river were making the music, too, but had to be told to flow, and the cushy clouds, as fat as blimps, required my encouragement.

Those were good days, back then, when I was a kid discovering meaningful music. Those were the days. But these are even better. Because these days I can play *Finlandia* myself. What happened was, my lady bought me twenty piano lessons for Christmas. I was so shocked by this present it took me nearly a year to recover and get up the guts to go. Like so many people in middle age, I had reached that point where I didn't really want to do anything I wasn't already good at. But I finally humbled myself and went.

Am I glad I did. I've still got dumb thumbs and fumblefingers, but I can make music nevertheless. Every day I come home when my family is out so I can strike sour notes without worry and fully indulge my repetition compulsion. The amazing thing is, I can't wear out *Finlandia*. Like a great poem or classic short story, this pagan hymn feels fresh each time I play it through. Each time it gives me joy.

But I'm already middle-aged! Too late for a concert career. Too late to become a composer now. Too late, at this date, to ever be anything more than a plunker. Which leaves me free, I guess. I play for sheer, pure pleasure. I play to ease myself through winter. And I play, apparently, to honor the dead. For they crowd close behind me, a silent choir, whenever I play for long. I play, first of all, in honor of Jan Sibelius, the dead man who discovered this miraculous combination of notes. But my mother is nearby, too, pleased that I'm learning to play at long last, relieved that she no longer has to plead with me to practice. And my Finnish grandpa, who loved the schottische, he's often here. And I see my grandmother again, laboring and laughing at the old pump organ, her style frightful, her elbows flying.

But most of all, it seems, I play for the suicides. I play to honor that tired old lady, powdered and smelly, who taught me a year of piano when I was a boy. The poor thing traveled from one country school to another. And sometime later, I heard, she jumped off a bridge. Even Beethoven couldn't save her. I play for my pal who shot himself way back in our early thirties, who has missed out on the good and the bad of all these intervening years. And I play for the neighbor boy, who used to mow my lawn, who killed himself with a deer rifle out of some teenage despair. And I thank the music of the spheres that although I make a jillion mistakes at the old upright and everywhere else in my life besides, I never made *that* mistake. A few years back, in the midst of a midlife crackup, I came awfully close, but I didn't do it, I survived, and now, to my great surprise, I can play the piano! I can play *Finlandia! Finlandia* exists in several English versions, so it has more than one beginning: *This is my song, On great lone hills, Be still my soul.* But this morning I finally understand through and through what those opening chords really mean: *I am alive!*

ROUNDABOUT

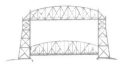

Cross-Country

One winter, when I was nine or ten, Jimmy Wetzler, the unofficial leader of our gang of savages, showed up on our sledding hill with a pair of skis. They were good, old-fashioned, wood, cross-country skis and came with bamboo poles. Jimmy wore white pants, a white wind jacket, and gauntlets that came to his elbows. This outfit was army surplus stuff, of which it seemed to me the Wetzler boys had an unfair, inexhaustible supply. Jimmy looked *completely* cool. He shuffled through the powdery drifts out to the crest of Miller's Hill, paused to answer a couple of our yapping inquiries, then launched himself straight down the hill. He went hissing toward the river; curved in a lazy, graceful arc; and slid along the riverbank till he finally came to a stop at the barbed wire fence that marked the edge of the pasture — twice as far as we'd ever gone on sleds or saucers. I couldn't believe it. Jimmy had looked so beautiful in that long, slow curve I wanted to hit somebody. Hot with jealousy, I clutched my orange fiberglass saucer like a shield and said, "Big deal. Who cares?"

That Christmas my brother and I received, as presents from our parents, matching pairs of red, wooden skis. They were basically boards with leather straps attached, through which you shoved the toes of your overshoes. Our skis were way too clunky to carry us far afield, but over the next couple of winters we had plenty of thrills and spills skiing down the sidehill in our yard.

By the time we were teenagers, the red clunkers had been abandoned. I didn't ski again until, as a senior at Southwest State, I signed up for a phy ed course in cross-country. Southwest State University is situated in the flatlands, but we had a zealous instructor in Jean Replinger, who hauled us around to every little hill and dale in the area. On our first weekend trip, I shot down a well-worn hill, hit a rut, and broke a ski. That afternoon, I went out again, ran into a tree root, and broke another ski. These were cheap wooden skis the school had bought by the gross, but my accomplishment was still impressive. Ten years later, I stopped in to visit Jean, and she pointed out my broken ski tips, crossed and hung above her desk with a note commemorating my peculiar feat, which no one else had equaled in all her years of teaching.

Maybe because I'd broken two skis in a single day I felt I didn't deserve to own a pair. Or maybe it was just that I spent my twenties in big cities. Or maybe — and this is what I really fear — maybe as a genetic Lutheran, I had to deny myself anything that gave me so much

pleasure. Whatever the irrational reason, I put off buy-
ing skis until I was thirty years old. One trip through
the woods and I knew that waiting so long for cross-
country skis was about the dumbest mistake I'd ever
made. Winter was changed for me forever.

By then I was living in the country. I could walk out
the door, step into my skis, shuffle half a mile across a
wind-whipped field, and catch a roller-coaster trail that
ran through shadowy oak woods for a mile and a half.
On Saturdays and Sundays, I had to watch for snowmo-
biles, but the rest of the week that trail was mine.
Usually I took my time, pausing to converse with squir-
rels or lob a snowball at a rabbit. Even though the
books all warned "Never ski alone!" I almost always did.
It's true that trail had scary runs with breakneck turns,
and I suppose I could have killed myself, but that was
part of the fun. And so was the silence, the whisper and
squeak of my skis, the chirr of my ski poles biting the
snow, the ragged sound of my own breathing. When
I broke back out of the woods, it was usually dusk. The
field sloped gently toward the house, and I could ride
the hard-packed drifts along the fenceline all the way
home. The sky was pink and blue. A few stars twinkled,
bright as icicles; the steeple of the Catholic church
pierced the horizon; yellow lights glowed in the houses
of the village. I felt as if I were skiing into a painting by
Van Gogh.

These days, in Duluth, I can't just step outside my
door to ski, but I've got four different trails less than ten
minutes away, and I try to ski at least three times a
week. I've become a kind of evangelist for this activity.
Fitness experts say the sport is one of the most efficient

forms of exercise. The setting for cross-country is almost always pretty. It's cheap. It's easy. The list of advantages seems endless. The other day I was out in the woods with a seven-year-old, who said, "You know what's really great about this winter skiing?"

I said, "No mosquitoes?"

"No mosquitoes," she agreed. "That's a good thing. But you know what's really great about it?"

"What?"

"You don't have to worry about bears. They're all asleep."

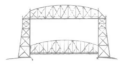

The Overcoat

Even though winters drag on too long up here in northern Minnesota, I'm always just a little sorry to see the season go. For one thing, I never seem to get my fill of cross-country skiing. For another thing, the onset of spring means I have to hang up my overcoat for months. I love my overcoat.

The proper winter coat is an essential survival item for any Minnesotan. As a kid I always wore a parka. During my college days I was cold a lot, getting by with various secondhand rags I can't remember now, although I *can* recall my greedy fantasies about a certain goose down parka that was supposed to be good to forty below. Never got that coat. But out in Boston, in my early twenties, I persuaded the friend of a friend who was in the navy to procure me a peacoat from the PX. I'd always admired them, and with good reason. I looked sharp in that wool jacket, and it kept me warm through a dozen winters. In these days of disposable goods that start to disintegrate before you get them halfway home, that peacoat seemed almost indestructible. I can still feel the comfort of the high, arching collar that kept the icy breezes off my neck. When the peacoat finally wore out, I moved on to cheap down parkas, but I've never been able to feel the same kind of affection for them — most likely because down coats inevitably give you what my stepdaughters call, disdainfully, "that puffy look."

I look better in my overcoat. I didn't own an overcoat till I was thirty-five, and, even then, I had to leave the country to buy one. I guess I'd always thought of overcoats as garb for older men — middle-aged, middle-class, ordinary folks. Whereas I, I was . . . something else . . . a young, bohemian, working-class, woodsy kind of guy. No overcoat for me. No thanks.

Before I knew it, I was halfway through my life. I found myself in Ireland, in winter, having supervised a group of college students with my wife all through the fall. Now the students had flown, and we were free at last. We were heading for Paris for Christmas and then a monthlong loop through Europe. What to wear? Already we'd encountered snow in Ireland, and we planned to pass through the Alps. We'd read warnings, too, about the cold mistral that comes blasting out of the mountains into the south of France. I had a nifty tweed sport coat I'd bought in Donegal, but I needed something more. Maybe an overcoat, I thought — a light, wool overcoat like my father used to wear.

When we hit Dublin I went shopping and discovered just the thing in Cleary's, a shop I later learned had been serving the Irish clergy for years. The overcoat was charcoal in color and, unlike any other coat I'd ever owned, came all the way down to my knees. The coat felt strange, but I liked it. I liked it a lot. I paid with the gorgeous money of that enlightened country, where they put poets on their currency instead of presidents. I wore the coat out of the shop, I remember, because it was a drizzly day. I remember the weather especially well because the splash of color I saw outside the shop was such a contrast to the gray. There, on the sidewalk, a woman was selling oranges, and the odd thing about it was — the small sort of weirdness you see in Ireland so often — the odd thing was, she was selling them out of a baby buggy. She had a baby buggy piled high with oranges, and there, in that wet weather, the oranges absolutely blazed.

I wish I'd bought one of those oranges, I've thought of them so often since. But I was preoccupied with a far greater strangeness. As I strode down the glistening street in my new overcoat, I was feeling unreasonably happy, elevated somehow, and transformed. This peculiar gladness had come over me the minute I'd put on the overcoat inside the store. It wasn't dissipating, either, but growing more intense. Suddenly I understood. I had become my father.

I was flooded then with mental photos of my father in his prime. I saw him digging out the car back in those winters when we lived on the Canadian border, when the heavens opened in October and snowed incessantly till May. I saw him heading out the door, his robes across one arm, on one of those interminable Sundays when he drove up north to serve the Indian churches way back in the woods. I saw him hunched on the sidelines of the football field, where he'd come to watch me play. I saw him standing by my mother, her arm looped through his, about to go somewhere without me. All these pictures came to me, quite naturally, in black-and-white. In every one, my father wore his overcoat.

Well. I'd known that clothes could make a difference. I'd found out, for example, that if I wore a sport coat and tight shoes to school, my language in the classroom grew more careful and precise. But I'd never experienced anything like this. Somehow when I donned that overcoat in Cleary's, I put on the mantle of an older man — my father, maybe, maybe the man I might turn out to be, with luck, somewhere down the line — responsible, confident, and kind. At the time, I knew that I was just pretending. All the hard stuff lay ahead, without my knowing it — trouble with liquor and women, therapy, divorce, remarriage, family life. But the overcoat had brought me a presentiment that middle age would actually hold the joy that's falsely advertised for youth. If the coat had made me feel stodgy, I'm sure I would have shucked it in a flash. But that wasn't the case. No, as I strolled down the street in my new overcoat, I felt, for the first time, finally, grown up.

That coat from Cleary's has served me well through ten cold winters. I've noticed the lining needs to be resewn, but otherwise I don't see why my overcoat won't last me ten more years, because I don't dress up that much. Yet every time I get the chance, every time I slip into those silky sleeves, I feel I'm about to step into a black-and-white movie from the forties. I'm still so delighted by my overcoat I sometimes think, How about a hat?

I don't guess anyone can see how strange I feel when I put on my overcoat. I look fairly ordinary: a middle-aged, middle-class guy who's going gray. But it feels extraordinary to exit a theater, say, and help my wife into her coat and shrug into my own. As I fumble with the buttons, I'm apt to think of my father, who has Alzheimer's now, who can't find the sleeve of his coat or fasten his buttons himself. I see I have his hands. I'm surprised by my new wedding band and wonder, Who's this woman in the deep red coat who smiles up at me with wrinkles around her eyes? And who am I, I wonder, as I stand there in my overcoat. We could be characters in a play. She seems to know me, though, and so I offer her my arm, and we walk into the great and overwhelming night that is our life.

Map Fishing

These days, when I hear folks express their fears that winter's never going to end, when others groan incessantly about the dirty snow, I just nod and grin. Midwinter used to make me gloomy, too, but several years ago I found a sport to keep my spirits up until the birds come back. This indoor hobby will sustain me for three months but not one moment more. I resist it through the long nights of November, the dark days of December, the bitter, interminable hours of January. But along about February, I let myself go map fishing at last.

Call it creative visualization or self-delusion, but map fishing maintains the fragile mental health of many Northerners who otherwise would go insane by March. The necessary gear is minimal; a selective memory and a feverish imagination are nearly enough. But you do need a map. A state highway map will fit the bill for most beginners, but experienced indoor fishermen own highly detailed charts that provide full coverage of their favorite areas. I've got about two dozen. I like to do my summer fishing by canoe, so most of my maps focus on the Boundary Waters of northern Minnesota and Quetico Provincial Park, just across the border. My kind of fisherman is presented with three possibilities: the yellow maps manufactured by the Fisher Company (promising name!), the green and blue ones issued by the U.S. Geological Survey, and the blue and white ones by McKenzie. For my money, and I don't have much, your best bet for fishing both indoors and out is the blue and white beauties by McKenzie. The colors may seem a bit too reminiscent of the winter scene you're trying to escape, but the contour lines will tell you if the lake you're dreaming over is backed by hills or surrounded by a swamp. The McKenzie maps are also waterproof. That's how you can recognize them in the store: look for the lunatic cartoon character in the checkered shirt, declaring, "Gosh, I can't tear this map even in the rain!"

I recommend reserving a large desk or table for map fishing expeditions. That way you'll avoid the backache and carpet burns so often suffered by newcomers to this exciting sport, who naively spread their maps out on the floor. You might want to augment your maps with books on nature, campcraft, or the habits of the fish you most prefer, but these are optional. Myself, I find the county fishing guides quite stimulating. The author of my guide to Lake County is a master of the tantalizing comment. He writes, for example, of Tofte Lake, outside of Ely: "Nice trout, good fishing. Some can't catch 'em." You might want to keep your tackle close at hand. I find that fingering a silver spoon or spinner does wonders for my fantasies. I also like to give my dreaming some direction with my compass. When the trees are all bare naked and the good earth buried underneath two feet of snow, it's nice to see that arrow, live and quivering, still pointing toward those places I love most. Reassuring somehow. Good old north.

So here I sit, brooding like God above a piece of northern Minnesota and a slice of southern Canada, all of it marbled with a thousand lakes and rivers. Where should we go? Three lakes in a row provide the chance to practice my Ojibway: Ogishkemuncie, Gabimichigami, Kekekabic. A few of these lakes must have been named for laughs: Dumbbell, for example. Poobah. Hey! Here's one with my name on it. Bart Lake. I'll have to check that out. But first I'm going back to fish that bass lake on the border. It's a muggy afternoon in August, we've just watched an osprey get up off its nest, and now we're paddling that shallow channel at the west end of the lake. Holy cats! Did you see that? Stunned, we sit frozen in the boat as a hundred smallmouth bass flow past in a mere two feet of water. There among them, like a wolf among the sheep, slides a muskie, two feet long. Then he's gone. But the bass fan out in a broad, transparent pool, and we can see them rise to take our lures. This is like fishing an aquarium, unbelievable but true.

The real beauty of map fishing is that anything is possible. You can easily rerun a dreamy memory like that one or take a trip that's never going to happen. Make my father fifty-five again, and I'll guide him to the rainbow trout he never caught. Let me take my dead friend Joe to north Ontario. Since Joe had such

a genius for friendship, always took great joy in other
people's pleasure, I can let myself catch all the fish.
Or say I'm not divorced, I haven't wrecked my first
marriage yet. Forget the rough water, the awful fight
we had on our way to this secluded lake. Put me in the
stern again, my wife up in the bow, and let her grumble
how she never catches anything. I'll point out the swirl
below the rapids. Let her make a lovely cast. And now
I'm on my knees in the bottom of the boat, gasping
with laughter as I unhook her two-pound bass, and she
cries once more with triumph and surprise: "Hey!
I caught a fish! I caught a fish!"

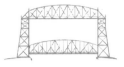

God's Own Ice Rink

As Shakespeare might have said, "That time of year thou mayst now behold / When it ought to be warm, but it's still darn cold." Officially it's spring, but you couldn't prove that in Duluth. Up here at the top of the map, we're still locked in a world of ice. We've seen some sunny days, all right, and even a green blade of grass or two, but the ground remains hard as iron, we're still scraping ice off the windshields, and the streets are edged with ridges of dirty gunk that looks like volcanic rock. Is there any way to appreciate this lousy, in-between season?

Well, I try to remember that ice is a precious commodity down at the equator. I recall that my grandparents had an icebox rather than a refrigerator and stored blocks of ice under sawdust late into the summer. Such mental effort eases my resentment of that hard stuff in the yard. But when it comes right down to the butt-end of winter, I often have to take direct action. So I'll drive out along the North Shore to watch the Coast Guard cutter *Sundew* try to break a shipping lane through miles of ice. I'll keep my eye out, too, for the dazzling slag heaps of pale blue ice that pile up along the shore as the sheet breaks up and wind drives it onto the beaches. It looks like light blue quartz, like something we ought to mine or display in museums. Such tactics help, but a few years back Lake Superior froze over completely, and some folks were predicting we wouldn't be ice-free until June. By late March, I was desperate.

Finally I decided, what the heck, might as well make the most of it. I'd been skiing all winter, but I hadn't laced my skates once. The snow had pretty much melted or blown off the big lake. It looked like God's own ice rink out there, so I thought I'd go for a spin. I dug my rusty hockey skates out of the basement and stopped at the hardware store for a couple of ice picks. Ice picks? Well, yeah, I'd read something somewhere. If you fall through the ice, this article said, your biggest problem is going to be getting a grip in order to haul yourself out. Therefore, those who venture out on thin ice ought to carry a pair of ice picks. Made sense to me.

I drove up the shore until I saw the first cluster of shacks and dark figures far out on the lake. Crazy people. Ice fishermen. Now, I'm an avid fisherman myself, but I confine my obsession to summer. Standing around out in the cold all day to not catch fish has always struck me as a very weird sport. But I thought it would be a good idea to make that little ice fishing village my goal. I thought if those nuts out there hadn't sunk I ought to be safe. On the other hand, a few ice fishermen fall in or float away on ice floes every year, so I knew there weren't any guarantees.

I stumbled down the bank, crunched across some shards of broken ice, and sloshed through three inches of water. Not a good sign. Teetering on one blade at a time, I removed my skate guards. I put one ice pick in each front pocket. Was this a good idea? Probably not, but what the hell. I shoved off.

If this was God's ice rink, He'd done a lousy job of flooding it. The surface was pocked with air bubbles and wrinkled with ripples. It wasn't quite as bad as skating on a washboard, but close. Still, I could scoot along all right, except that every now and then I ran out of black ice. I'd come to a patch of brittle, white ice that broke beneath my feet like egg shells. I took choppy steps and stumbled forward until I hit black ice again. After a hundred yards of this herky-jerky progress, I came to the first of the crazy people, a pair of ice fishermen who hadn't had a single bite. They didn't have a house, either. They'd been standing around in piles of clothes all afternoon, drinking beer and watching their holes. This was fun for them. They were pretty amused to see somebody out there on skates. We had a nice chat, and then I said I was heading out as far as those fishermen who looked like little silhouettes off there in the distance. "How far is that, would you guess?" "Mile and a half," they said, "two miles. Those guys are crazy."

I skated off and tried to follow the meandering pattern of black ice, to avoid the brittle stuff. I wished I'd worn a hat. The sky was brilliant, but the breeze was brisker out here than back on shore. I passed a blue tent.

I passed a fisherman perched on his red four-wheeler.
I stopped to rest. My legs were jittery from skating on
such a lumpy surface. I pushed on, though, and the little fishermen grew larger. I stumbled often now, and
felt like an idiot. The ice was two feet thick. I wasn't
going to break through. But I could easily stumble, fall,
and drive the damn ice picks into my thighs. I could
have carried the picks in my hands, I suppose, but I was
already carrying my skate guards, and besides, I was
ashamed to let the fishermen see how stupid I had been.

Weak in the knees and sore in the ankles, I arrived at
the farthest cluster of fishermen. There were three of
them, and they had drilled their holes along a pressure
ridge where the ice had buckled. Two of them had shel-
ters. I skated up to the other guy, a tall, sturdy fellow
dressed in a dirty snowmobile suit. "Any luck?" I asked.
Nothing all day, the man said, though his friends had
had a few bites. His name was Don, and he chose to
ignore the fact that I was on skates. Don had two fishing poles laid out on the ice with heavy line running
down into 170 feet of cold water. He stood with his
back to those holes, and while we talked, he worked
another hole with a handheld rig. Suddenly I noticed
one of the rods jump a bit. "Say," I said, "I think you've
got something there." Don spun around, and both of us
watched — frozen, struck dumb — as the pole skidded
across the ice, tipped straight up, and disappeared
down the hole. For several seconds, neither one of us
could speak. Some hefty lake trout had caught himself
a hundred-dollar fishing rod. With plenty of advice from
his pals, Don sank a heavy lure down the hole, hoping
to snag the lost line and retrieve rod and lunker both,

but this was not to be. Don blamed himself, since he'd forgotten to take off the drag, but I felt as if I'd brought the man bad luck, so I skated away to the sound of the fishermen drilling more holes with their ice auger, still hoping to fish up Don's pole.

"Wow," I thought as I skated toward shore, "ice fishing is even dumber than I figured." But I liked being out there on the ice. Halfway back, I stopped and lit up one of the small cigars I allow myself every once in a while. My legs felt rubbery, but I wondered, "What if a guy were in shape? Say the lake froze over again next year, and you watched it closely and caught some smooth ice. Could you throw a thermos in a backpack — coupla oranges, coupla Snickers — and skate up as far as Two Harbors? Or, hey, maybe clear across to Cornucopia? Or would that be too crazy?" Such were a few of my thoughts on a bright blue day at the end of March in the endless winter of '94, as I skated the bumpy ice of Lake Superior about a mile out from shore, ice picks in my pockets, skate guards in my hands, a stinky, short cigar between my teeth.

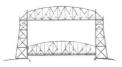

Boundary Waters Canoe Park

Every spring I go after lake trout. There's an old saying that the lake trout will be biting when the birch leaves are the size of beavers' ears, but I never seem to have a beaver handy when the time comes, so I can only guess. I *have* developed three reminders to help me plan my trips: Avoid the fishing opener. Avoid Memorial Day weekend. Go before the first of June. When I can keep those simple rules, my spring trip often turns out to be the best of the year. The fish are dumb and hungry. The woods are still bug-free. And the traffic in the Boundary Waters — the most popular wilderness area in the country — remains relatively light in May. This last point is an important consideration if, like me, you're not really happy unless you've got an entire lake to yourself.

Unfortunately, I sometimes have to break my own rules. One year I couldn't get away until Memorial Day weekend, and this meant trouble when I went down to the Forest Service office to reserve my travel permit. The permits, which keep the Boundary Waters from being completely overrun, are a necessary evil, but they make me mad anyhow. When I was a kid, you just packed up your stuff and went into the woods. Nowadays you have to pay good money down and make a reservation as if you were planning to pitch your tent inside a damned hotel. And, naturally, the entry points I wanted were already taken — for Thursday, Friday, Saturday. I'd have to wait clear until Sunday for the privilege of sleeping on the ground. Thus began a slow burn that grew hotter the closer I came to what the Forest Service likes to call "your wilderness experience."

For one thing, I got mad all over again at what the Department of Transportation has done to Silver Cliff. A few years back they blew a hole through it, and now they brag that we have the only hardrock tunnel in the entire Midwest. Big deal. As far as I can see, it's a hole in a hill, lined with bathroom tile. I call it the Culvert. Just like that, they ruined one of the most majestic hunks of rock in the whole state. I *understand* the curve around the cliff was creepy, less than safe. So what? It's *good* for people to be scared by nature. I *understand* there was a serious problem with erosion. But was blowing a hole through Silver Cliff the only solution? How come I never got to vote on this? Who decided we should trade our most spectacular highway view of Lake Superior for a quarter-mile of bathroom tile? Talk about tunnel vision! And they did the same damn thing to Lafayette Bluff!

Fuming and depressed, I chugged into Grand Marais, where I stopped to pick up my permit and found myself subjected to another indignity devised by the Forest

Service. I, Bart Sutter, woodsman extraordinaire; veteran canoeist; reader of Ed Abbey, Sig Olson, and the *Boy Scout Handbook*; I, Chingachgook; *I* was required to watch a video on camping etiquette, as if I were some twelve-year-old from Dallas or Chicago. What could I do but talk back? When the TV spoke of clean water, I argued that the lakes were full of mercury. When the narrator insisted on calling this region the Boundary Waters Canoe Area *Wilderness*, I said, "Pah! This ain't no wilderness. This is a goddamned park, the Boundary Waters Canoe Park." When the Forest Service clerk made me take a little quiz on garbage, bears, and fire grates, I nearly spit. Nor was I especially pleased to arrive at my favorite backwoods entry point and find a half dozen — count 'em, six — cars pulled up in the brush ahead of me. I almost turned for home. But no, I shouldered my canoe and started up the trail, hotheaded, thinking, as I do each year, I'm done with the Boundary Waters, thinking, desperately, of our wild neighbor to the north, singing, furiously, under the canoe: "*O, Canada!* Hm-hm, hm-hm, hm-hm!"

But once I'd got by the rubble at Silver Cliff, once I'd run the bureaucratic gauntlet, once I finally made it out on the lakes, I had a fine time. I went in four lakes and had the last one to myself. My sleeping bag was flimsy, and I shivered through the night, but I heard loons, I saw an osprey, and I caught five trout, the best I'd ever done. The fishing wasn't fast, exactly, but each time I was just about to quit, I caught one. Lakers are beautiful fish, mottled green and white, washed with pink and blue. When I opened these, their flesh glowed bright orange, like some exotic fruit, and tasted sweet as salmon. The last one I caught weighed two and a half pounds, and to me, a mediocre fisherman, it looked like a shark. I was very happy as I drove the gravel road back toward Grand Marais. And I was not surprised when, rumbling down a hill and through a marsh, I saw a great gray owl — big as an eagle, symbol of true wilderness — perched on a fence post, regarding me with large, yellow eyes. I didn't stop. I drove right on but knew that I'd be back. Maybe the Boundary Waters isn't really wilderness, but it's still a damn nice park.

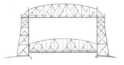

Dream Canoe

In the beginning, all my canoe trips were imaginary.
I grew up in motorboat country — southern Minnesota,
northern Iowa — but even as a kid I knew I was meant
for quieter craft. The first canoes I encountered weren't
made of metal or wood, they were made of words: the
canoe Huck found floating down the Mississippi in
Huckleberry Finn, the birchbark classics described by
James Fenimore Cooper in *The Leatherstocking Tales*. In
high school I discovered the books of Sigurd Olson
and grew permanently homesick for the Boundary
Waters, a place where I had never been. I hung a map
of Minnesota on my bedroom wall and daydreamed
I was shooting rapids, fighting headwinds, drifting still,
deep waters, listening to loons.

The first actual canoe in which I ever set foot
belonged to a boy named Dick Knight. Dick was about
the only other kid in the state who regularly sent in observations to *Iowa Bird Life*, and as two lonely, precocious

ornithologists, we'd struck up a correspondence. Dick's dad was a professor of entomology — a bug man — and the summer I was fifteen, Dick's family was living at a research station on Spirit Lake. One day, when we were in the area, I persuaded my dad to stop in for a quick visit. Now, nearly thirty years later, all I remember of that afternoon is the canoe ride.

Dick's canoe was a wonderful, old-fashioned job with varnished wood inside and a green canvas hull. I settled myself uneasily in the bow. Dick launched the canoe and perched on the stern deck plate, showing off. It seemed awfully tippy to me, but we didn't capsize, and after a minute or two I relaxed enough to enjoy the new sensations. I might have been sitting astride a dolphin, the canoe felt so alive. It quivered like a wild animal, but Dick had it under control, and we moved smoothly across the bay.

The canoe surged ahead when Dick dug in with his paddle, and then, like a held breath let loose, the canoe would glide through the golden water. Surge, and glide. Surge, and glide. Here was a hammock that moved. The motion was well-oiled, too — so smooth it seemed we were not only on the water or in it but somehow we were it, though, really, of course, we were just passing through. This magnificent, magisterial form of locomotion instantly became my favorite mode of transportation, and so it remains, matched only by the swoop and glide of cross-country skiing and the dreamy feel of a train pulling out of the station.

It was a hot day back there in northern Iowa, but a light breeze riffled my hair. Behind my back, Dick was talking, but I only caught snatches of what he was saying. Canoes, though quiet, are not conducive to conversation; the distance between bow and stern is exactly wrong. I heard Dick say something about someone doing research on diatoms, the single-celled algae that lived in the lake. But given the giddy state I was in, "diatoms" became "diamonds," because I was dazzled, gazing down and down through the glittering green-gold water. A red-winged blackbird protested when we came too near her nest on the far shore, so we swung around, and soon we were back where we'd begun. My first real canoe trip had lasted a mere twenty minutes, but when I stepped out on the dock I was somebody else. One thing I knew for sure: someday I would own my own canoe.

Sad to say, it was twenty-two years before I felt I could make that purchase. In the meantime, though, I rented, borrowed, and begged. When I was nineteen I had the use of a friend's lightweight Grumman, and I stayed the summer at a trapper's cabin in Canada, twenty miles from the nearest road. That canoe had been fixed with pop rivets, it was dinged all over with dents, and I couldn't have been happier with it. One year I lived on a little lake near St. Cloud, Minnesota, where I commandeered the landlord's battered old Alumacraft for my private purposes, which were (1) aimlessly drifting about, and (2) fishing for northerns along the weedline. I've paddled plastic tubs and portaged canoes made of space-age materials you could see through. I might prefer one to another, but they've all provided that magical surge and glide, and so, at bottom, they've all seemed to me mysteriously somehow the same.

And that's why I'm nuts about canoeing still. It takes me into the dreamtime — that weird inner space where the past and future interpenetrate. Not long ago I was paddling the loveliest canoe into which I have ever settled my butt — a handmade, cedar-strip boat built by an architect. That wood sculpture was a pleasure to behold, to sit in and maneuver. But the rockabye motion was much the same as what I'd felt in Iowa when I was fifteen. And this backwoods lake, one of my favorites, hadn't changed a whit from the previous year. Maybe it was always spring up here, the granite hills softened by the tender pastels of deciduous trees bursting their buds. The water was black and silver still, and the blue lake trout I brought aboard could have been the one I caught the year before. I put the fish on the stringer, picked up my paddle, and dipped it in silver. I had no idea where I was.

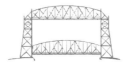

The Next Best Thing to Nobody

One lucky year, when I checked the calendar for my annual lake trout trip, my eyes bugged out. The fourth week in May was completely free. Instead of nibbling at the edge of the Boundary Waters on a long weekend, I could really go somewhere. I decided on a route with lots of options and the provisional goal of reaching a body of water at the heart of the BWCA, which, for purposes of public communication, I'm going to call Eagle Lake. I believe that honesty is the best policy for everything except blueberry patches and fishing spots.

As soon as I'd chosen a route, I nailed down a reservation. Deciding on a partner took more time. It isn't easy, in middle age, to find someone willing and able to steal a week away from work and family. What's more, I've done so much canoe camping by now that I've grown persnickety about my partners. I don't want a wimp, and I don't want a maniacal macho man. I don't want a drunk or a babbler. I don't want a grump or a

whiner. As I ran through my list of possible partners ...
my brother was busy, Louis loved to fish but hated
camping, Jim would still be teaching school ... I kept
coming back to Tom.

Tom is a quiet, steady guy with a wry sense of humor.
I'd shared an office with him a few years back, and we'd
taken a shine to each other. I'd never been in the woods
with him, but I had a hunch he'd be just right. Besides,
he'd invited me on a trip the year before, which I'd had
to refuse, so I figured he figured I was okay. It's a deli-
cate business, this picking a fishing partner.

When I called him with my proposal, Tom turned
me down with a groan of regret; he was already committed to a trip that week. But the next day he called to
ask if he could still come along. He had decided to
back out of the other trip and rearrange his schedule in
order to go with me. Was I flattered. Why had he
changed his mind? Well, he couldn't resist the chance
to see this new country on the route I'd mapped out.
Besides, he thought I'd make a fine partner. He'd been
out with plenty of guys over the years, but way too
many of them just couldn't seem to stop talking. That
wasn't why he went into the woods, to listen to somebody's monologue. He'd thought about this a lot, Tom
said. He felt he knew me fairly well, and he figured
I was the next best thing to nobody.

I didn't know whether to take this as praise or an
insult, but it made me laugh. I decided to take it as a
compliment, and after our week in the woods I knew
I was right. In fact, I wouldn't mind having that phrase
carved on my tombstone: Here lies Barton Sutter, the
Next Best Thing to Nobody.

That *is* why we go to the woods, isn't it — to get away from others? Hell, said Jean-Paul Sartre, is other people. Of course if you truly love solitude above all else, you'll wade out into the Big Bog north of Red Lake, where you'll encounter nobody but black flies. Or you could just lock yourself in your room. But that's not quite what you had in mind, was it? No, you're after a certain sort of aesthetic experience that includes fresh fish, the rockabye motion of a canoe, the scent of cedar trees, et cetera. If that's what you want, though, and you want to be alone, then why not just go solo?

Well, I do that — fairly often. I think going alone is about the best way to spend time in canoe country. But solo travel is awfully hard work. Your speed is cut by two-thirds, and with nobody sharing the chores, you work from dawn to dark. So most people, most of the time, look for partners. I know two brothers who solve this dilemma by traveling together in the same canoe but pretending they're alone. They talk no more than necessary, and when they make camp they build differ-ent fires to cook their meals and they sleep in separate tents. To each his own, as the saying goes, but that arrangement does strike me as a weensy bit nuts.

There's a natural kind of dual solitude, though. It's the sort of steady state that sometimes develops in a lucky marriage, in which a pair can be alone together without feeling lonesome, in which much is understood without speech, in which silences are calm, deep, and satisfying. Some such quiet understanding develops quickly between like-minded partners out on the canoe trails: If you gather firewood, I'll fetch the water. If you cook supper, I'll do the dishes. You paddle on the left,

I'll paddle on the right. There's no need to negotiate . . . or even to speak.

Tom and I proved to be lucky that way. Since we both have a high regard for silence, we traveled in a kind of luxurious quiet. Such peace is hard to come by these days. The noise of our infernal machinery is nearly omnipresent; clocks and refrigerators hum in our sleep. But the silence of canoe country is more than lack of racket. Silence is not the absence of sound. True silence is spacious and easily includes the splatter of waves, the song of the wind, the jabber of warblers in the high treetops. Sometimes it even seems to contain the glistening yellow of buttercups, the fragrance of wild roses. Silence, as the Quakers know, is never nothing, but a positive force, mysterious, sacred, and profound. Out of deep silence, it has always seemed to me, comes the best of what we know — poetry, music, the most moving conversations.

Tom and I had some terrific talks on our trip, in part because we traveled through so much silence. On portage breaks, around the evening fire, we talked about campcraft and earlier trips we had taken. We talked about trouble with booze and drugs. We talked about women and children and work. Backcountry campers always talk about food, but we came back to that topic again and again because Tom had cancer, and he was treating it with diet. We'd hauled along fresh fruits and vegetables, all sorts of things most go-light campers reject. Tom's diet seemed to be working — his cancer count was down — but the fact of his disease sure affected the way I saw the landscape. Instead of already scheming my next trip through this country, and so being neither here nor there, I saw things more as I imagined Tom did: here and now, here now, this tree, this rock, this hawk.

Spending time with a man who has cancer sobers you up and gives you perspective. Thinking how near Tom was to being nobody reminded me of my own precarious hold on life and the title Tom had given me, the Next Best Thing to Nobody. Oddly enough, as the trip went on, the notion of "nobody" began to take on personality, to become not nothing but a positive force, like silence. What can I say? Wild country gives you wild ideas.

After three days, we were closing in on Eagle Lake. Travel had been slow but steady, and we'd caught big fish. Our one disappointment was that we'd seen other people on every lake. Now we hoped to leave them behind. We portaged into a bog and followed a narrow, winding creek for nearly an hour until the banks grew so tight the canoe got stuck. I traced several trails up a hillside through the trees, but they all petered out. We were less than half a mile away, but we could not find the portage into Eagle Lake. After coming all this way! Finally Tom volunteered to walk what looked like a moose trail through the swamp. He left me fuming and defeated, puffing a cigar, fighting flies, and trickling sweat. I was down, way down. But Tom was back in half an hour. "I found it," he told me.

"What?"

"The portage. And the lake. It's beautiful. But some-body's there."

There was no real choice, of course. Tom had a peculiar, satisfied gleam in his eye as he hoisted a pack on his back. "I haven't done anything this insane," he said, "since I was eighteen." We slogged off through the swamp, and an hour later we had humped the canoe and all our gear across the bog, up the hill through the woods, around the switchbacks, over deadfalls, through the brush to the smooth rock shelf on the edge of Eagle Lake. We stood stunned with exhaustion and looked out at the lake. Late afternoon light came gleaming through the goldgreen leaves of birch and aspen, and the lake, ringed round with hills, looked bluer than the sky. The place felt like the top of the world. Plus, the people who'd been on the lake were heading out. They'd only come in on a day trip from another camp. As soon as they were out of sight, Tom and I exchanged a high five.

We loaded the canoe and drifted out over the depths. The water was shockingly cold, like liquid ice. The light was gold. Ahead of us, lake trout broke the surface like small, dark dolphins. The silence seemed deeper than the lake itself, and we rejoiced. This was what we'd come for. Nobody was here.

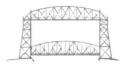

Falcon, Eagle, Snake

Jim, John, and I were guiding four kids on an easy trip through the Boundary Waters. With a ratio of nearly one parent per teenager, the odds looked good for keeping the kids in line. The weather forecast was favorable, too. But the most promising sign appeared in the sky just as we were setting up camp our first night out. John gave a holler, and we all looked up to see a falcon chase a bald eagle over the neighboring island. From the talons of the eagle dangled a snake. What an omen! I felt as if I'd suddenly stepped into a hexagram of the *I Ching*: falcon, eagle, snake. Where power is great, there is also great danger. He who exercises equal measures of courage and caution shall cross the wide water. There will be good fortune.

Aside from some unexpected rain, we did have good luck on this outing. Oh, once we forgot a fishing rod and had to double back. But nobody capsized, nobody drowned, nobody took a hook in the head. The kids

avoided major spats and only required the lightest
reminders to do their chores. They were fun and made
me proud, but in many ways it was clear that these people in their early teens were on a separate trip, as, I suppose, the different generations always are. They
seemed happy to keep to themselves for hours on end,
playing cards in the tent, practicing their dirty words,
laughing and laughing. Good golly, how they giggled.
One night as Jim and I lay drifting toward sleep, the
girls fell into such an extended, exquisite laughing fit
that we went into convulsions ourselves, just listening
to them yelp and titter.

But my most interesting good luck on this trip came
in the form of my adult companions. It would be hard
to imagine two men more different from each other
than John and Jim. John is dark and stocky, a forest
ecologist with a beard to match his Ph.D. Jim is
smooth-shaven, a tall, balding redhead who works as a
rural mail carrier and also teaches tai chi. John's manner
is focused, serious, concerned. Jim's is dreamy, twinkling, more than half-amused. Canoe trips are always
an education, but it was especially entertaining and
instructive to have such different men for company.

John was a fount of information, spouting scientific
as well as common names for plants and animals, pointing out differences between species, supplying us with
nice reminders for identifying trees — how the black
spruce tapers toward the top like a candle, for example,
while the white pine spreads out like a candelabra. John
was a great camp worker, too: chopping wood, organiz-
ing equipment, and serving as chief engineer for the
nightly food-pack hangings. I was especially grateful

for this last ability because I'm so lousy at stringing up a food pack that, personally, I've about quit trying. The idea, of course, is to suspend the pack from a tree in such a manner that a bear can't get at it. Usually, by the time I finish playing rope-a-dope, the sagging food pack looks like easy pickings for an unambitious chipmunk, never mind a hungry bear. Or else I get the rope so tangled in the branches that all I can do is cut the line. Over the years, I've left enough rope hanging in the Boundary Waters to furnish a small hardware store. I was pleased and relieved to hand this challenge to someone with a better understanding of basic physics than mine.

One of the most interesting things I learned from John was how to recognize a fire scar. Fire scars have a vaginal shape and are smooth in the middle, where flames burned down to bare wood. Such a scar looks a lot like an old blaze cut in a tree trunk to mark a trail, but it's usually longer and closer to the ground. You can tell which direction the fire came from because the flames curl around the trunk and create the scar on the downwind side. I'd seen fire scars all my life without recognizing them for what they were. Suddenly I had a whole new way to read the forest.

Talk of forest fires gave John the chance to tell us about his hero, Bud Heinselman. I'm sorry to say I'd never heard of Heinselman, who died in 1993, though John and others argue that Heinselman, more than any other person, was responsible for preserving the Boundary Waters. For nearly thirty years, Heinselman worked as a research ecologist for the U.S. Forest Service. He never published for a general audience, which probably explains why he's less well known than someone like Sigurd Olson. But in the scientific community, Heinselman is a legend, and his fire history of the Boundary Waters is a classic in ecology.

What impressed me most in the story of Bud Heinselman was that after thirty years in the Forest Service he felt so angered by the agency's disregard of wilderness values that he quit. Taking early retirement, he helped form the Friends of the Boundary Waters and gave himself to the campaign that culminated in the 1978 BWCA Wilderness Act. He was hung in effigy alongside Sigurd Olson at the congressional field hearings in Ely. He and his wife lived in Washington for several years in order to lobby legislators. With his deep sincerity, his intimate knowledge of the Boundary Waters, and his intriguing maps of the area, Heinselman proved irresistible.

I was very pleased to learn about this dead man, this friend I never knew I had. And I was horrified to learn from John that my own congressman, James Oberstar, was introducing legislation to undo Bud Heinselman's hard work. I was incredulous that here, at the close of the twentieth century, the most popular federal wilderness area in the country could still come under attack. But I was glad to get the bad news. It's not only good to know who your friends are; it's nice to know your enemies, too.

John was so full of fascinating information that I went away from the trip determined to read more, to study more deliberately. What I got from Jim was something subtler, harder to name, but equally important. Call it a resolution to enjoy my life more thoroughly.

I've seldom seen anyone so eager to welcome every moment, whatever it might bring. I'd like to know where Jim got this attitude, so I could go get some myself. I suspect he was born with a bunch of it. But I suspect, too, that Jim's apparent gratitude for each next minute has something to do with his having survived 365 days in Vietnam when each next minute might have been his last. And I'm sure his ability to say welcome, welcome to every new and same old thing also derives from his reading of Eastern philosophers and his daily practice of tai chi chuan, that graceful Chinese martial art that exercises body and soul alike.

Whatever its source, I found Jim's large enjoyment of life magnetically attractive — naturally enough, since for years I lived my life under the vague and gloomy idea that not only did God not exist, but He was out to get me. I pretty much agreed with Dorothy Parker: the one unfailing rule of the universe was that no matter how bad you expected things to be, they were sure to turn out worse. Slowly, gradually, in recent years I've been giving up this pathetic worldview. But it was shocking to spend so much time with someone like Jim, someone with such a radically different attitude.

I can still hear him gloating over the food as we dished up the evening meal. I can hear him yelp and bark and chatter with the kids as they played in the water like a family of otters. I can see him standing in his yellow rain suit, practicing tai chi like a ballet dancer whose only music was the falling rain. I remember Jim's crackpot proposal to swim the Boundary Waters with flippers, mask, and snorkel. I see him standing on the shore in the still of the evening, calling to the cliffs, "Hello!" And when the stone answered back, shouting out, "Ya wanna fight?" And when the cliffs called back, safely, from a distance, "Wanna fight? Wanna fight?" how Jim hollered, "Come here and say that!" and the cowardly cliffs could only repeat, "Come here and say that! Come here and say that!" Oh, but we laughed.

Each of these scenes holds a lesson for me about my sulky disposition. But maybe my favorite moment of the entire trip came at dusk one day when the lake went smooth as polished silver. Jim and I had each taken a canoe out and after paddling around on our own, coasting through the treetops reflected in the water, marveling at the almost mystical calm, we came together in a bay near camp, grinning and shaking our heads. When we finally spoke, we kept our voices hushed. I said, "I've been thinking about that story you told me about the Eskimos." Earlier Jim had said the Eskimos believed that sometimes the sea grew so calm and filled with such perfect reflections that a hunter could no longer tell water from sky and simply kayaked off into the heavens. Jim said, "Me, too. I'll tell you what. If you see me paddling off there above the tree-line, don't worry about me. I'll be okay."

It was a splendid trip, worthy of the omen we'd seen at the start. But there was one final incident some folks might call bad luck. Though we never saw a sign of bears the whole time we were out, when we landed back at the resort where we'd left our cars, we were stunned to discover that a bear had broken out the windows on the driver's side of both Jim's car and mine. We'd made the mistake of leaving them open a crack,

and there were paw prints on the dusty doors where
the bear had gotten up to tear the windows out. At first
I was dismayed, of course; but in the end I felt oddly
pleased, proud to drive around with bear tracks on my
door. Even as we stood there in the parking lot, survey-
ing the damage, we were able to laugh it off. "Next
time," John said, "we'll have to hang the cars in the
trees."

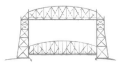

The Shrink-Wrapped Campfire

John Muir used to head off into the wilderness with little more than a tin cup and a loaf of bread. Today it's possible to spend a frightening amount of money on camping gear. I try to keep it simple, as Thoreau advised, but a glance at my equipment list for a typical trip . . . canoe, paddles, life jacket, tent, fly, sleeping bag, air mattress, sven saw, water bag . . . even a peek at my list makes it plain I've got plenty tied up in this stuff. I don't really mind. I'd rather have my money in camping gear than stuck in some bank that pays laughable rates. Yet I can't help but worry sometimes: have I become one of those despicable creatures who would rather buy camping equipment than camp?

Well, no . . . though I have to admit that browsing through sporting goods ranks right up there with loitering in a bookstore as my favorite shopping experience. And I can't begin to count the hours I've devoted to paging through the outdoor catalogs. I'd like to dignify that activity by calling it research, but it's really only daydreaming, the one sport for which I deserve an Olympic medal.

But I'm not alone. Building a personal outfit has been a dreamy, evolutionary process for most of the campers I know. As a kid, you fantasize about everything in the catalog but actually have to borrow most of your gear from your cousin. In your teens, you may own a basic outfit — tent, sleeping bag, cook kit, and pack — but it's probably clunky army surplus stuff. By the time you're into your twenties, you may have specialized (in back-packing, say, or canoeing), and the lifelong process of fine-tuning your gear has begun. Arguments among backcountry campers flare up like flames off of birch-bark. Goose down is lighter, but artificial fibers dry out faster if your sleeping bag gets wet. So which side are you on? Aluminum cook kits weigh less, but stainless steel heats more evenly. Which side are you on? Many campers concoct complex philosophies, complete with preposterous contradictions. A pair of my pals, who were otherwise ferocious about lightening their load, eventually included a cast-iron dutch oven in their cook kit because they liked the way it baked cakes.

After years of building your outfit, you may find yourself heading back in the other direction, subtract-ing rather than adding. Once upon a time, for example, I felt I had to pack along both ax and saw, as if, instead of going out to sleep in the forest, I meant to level it. By and by, I realized a hatchet, for half the heft, would accomplish all the work I wanted from the ax. Then I tried leaving the hatchet at home, having seen at last that my lightweight saw takes care of most of my

woodcutting needs. Someday, maybe, I'll be as wise as
my friend Steve, who goes off on canoe trips bare-
handed, knowing the only wood you really need you
can usually break across your knee.

Of course, if you carry the ideal of simplicity too far,
you'll walk off into the woods wearing nothing but bug
dope. This would be a mistake . . . and frightening for the
bears. The twentieth century has brought many worthy
innovations to backwoods camping — the nylon tent,
the goose down bag, the Kevlar canoe — and it's nutty
to ignore them. Personally, I feel the most remarkable
discovery in recent years has been made in the area of
breadstuffs. Used to be, you had to bake your own bread
on the trail (a tricky business), substitute crackers, or
squish a loaf of store-bought into a wad that you later
tried to pry apart like a damp, doughy accordion. But
lately we've been rescued by a product better known on
the streets of Manhattan than the canoe trails of the
North. I speak, of course, of the bagel. Of course! Chewy,
dense, compact, shockproof, even somewhat rain-resist-
ant, the bagel is the obvious solution to the camper's
need for bread. Why didn't we think of this before?
Well, we would have, but bagels are relatively new to
small towns in the Upper Midwest (I, for example, never
bit into a bagel until I was halfway into my twenties), and
besides, it takes time to see something so creatively, out
of its natural — in this case, urban — context. But now
there's no going back. I predict that by the turn of the
century, bannock and sourdough biscuits will be completely displaced by that marvel of marvels, the bagel.

I've been brooding hard about grub and gear because
I recently encountered a product that left me baffled

and breathless. I was up in Ely for some fishing one day
and stopped downtown for a burger. After lunch,
I decided to prowl through Piragis, the upscale camping store that sells everything from high-tech paddles
to dehydrated peas. Once again I was impressed by the
proliferation of outdoor products over the past twenty
years. There's a canoe for every preference, a book to
answer any question, and so many spectacular videos
you wonder why anyone bothers to leave the house.
I resisted the clever T-shirts. I laughed at the freeze-
dried foods. But I felt lucky to get out the door with
as little as I did: a fifty-foot coil of rope and a coffeepot
with a flip-top lid.

I left Piragis in a daze, stunned by the thing I had
seen. I had witnessed dozens of products I didn't
need — all attractively packaged — but the one thing
I didn't need most had left me numb with wonder. In
the back room, back by the nesting cook kits and
miniature stoves, I saw . . . a shrink-wrapped campfire.
I picked it up. I held it in my hands as if it might
explode. I turned it over and over and read the label
with care. The campfire measured something like eight
inches by five inches by two inches deep, and it came
in an open-faced, cardboard carton like those little blue
boxes in which berries are packed. This box, the label
assured me, was completely biodegradable and, like the
cellophane shrink-wrap that covered the campfire,
could be burned in the campfire. I can't quote the label
exactly, because I failed to purchase one of these fires,
but it was a work of art. The label presented the shrink-
wrapped campfire as an organic, environmentally sound
alternative to the messy camp stove. It promised that

the shrink-wrapped campfire would burn for forty-five
minutes, depending on conditions. The fire was said to
be sufficient to cook a meal for four to six persons. And
the label listed the contents of the campfire, as though
the carton were a packet of freeze-dried lasagne. The
major ingredients, as I recall, were wood, wood chips,
wood fiber, and bark. Several other ingredients were
listed, too, one of which might have been the scientific
name for paraffin or kerosene, but I can't say for sure.
Nor can I say how long I stood there turning that package in my hands. It looked to me like someone was selling a small box of wood scraps for $2.89, but the
package was so impressive I felt I must be missing
something. All you had to do to start the campfire,
the label declared, was to touch it with a match. The
match, oddly enough, was not included.

Tingling with astonishment, I stumbled from the
store and tried to forget what I had seen. Talk about
selling water by the river! Talk about an excrescence of
capitalism! Here was someone selling wood scraps to
campers who were about to set off into a wilderness of
how many billion trees? As I drove south out of Ely
through thousands of acres of wood, wood chips, wood
fiber, and bark, I tried to calm myself and think of other
things. But I couldn't help imagining a family from
Chicago, shopping for their first canoe trip, standing in
front of a stack of shrink-wrapped campfires, and making calculations: "Let's see, we'll be out seven days, times
three meals a day, plus a couple of fires at night . . . We
better take two dozen of these." I couldn't help but laugh.

But here's the horrific end to my story. By the time
I got home, two hours later, I knew that before the

summer was over I would have to go back to Piragis and purchase not one but a dozen shrink-wrapped campfires. I had to mail one to my smart-ass pal Joe, who last winter sent me a plastic package that was labeled "real artificial snow." And I wanted to hand-deliver a shrink-wrapped campfire to each of the most veteran campers I knew, just so I could watch their reactions. And I wanted one shrink-wrapped campfire all to myself. I would place it on the mantel as a conversation piece and symbol of late twentieth century American decadence. The shrink-wrapped campfire would serve as a kind of oracle, saying to me daily: "Be thou simple — even simple-minded. Above all, remember how little you need."

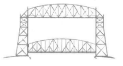

Dieback

My friend Phil, who is fast approaching the age of arthritis and wisdom, recently told his young son that of all living things, trees were his favorite. Birds came next, followed, he thought, by fish. Human beings, he told his boy, came in fourth at best. I was startled by this ranking but then both amazed and amused by the sympathy I felt for Phil's point of view. Trees didn't start World War II. Trees didn't kill six million Jews. The history of this demented century — or even a glimpse of the evening news — is enough to make you turn away from mankind in disgust and seek the company of something clean, green, and graceful.

The affection people feel for trees — which are members, after all, of a completely different kingdom — is quite remarkable. There's a tall box elder in my boyhood that I recall more fondly than several of my uncles. I know a woman who, stuck in a terrible marriage, planted an entire orchard of flowering trees in order to give herself hope. I know another who, badly abused by an older brother during her girlhood on a lonesome northern farm, took the birch trees as her friends. She, who became a scientist — a mild, rational woman — shrieked like a banshee when her husband recently suggested they should cut the big old birches that are dying in their yard.

Birches are dying all over northern Minnesota now — in yards and parks, along the North Shore, way back in the woods. Their leaves are going yellow in midsummer. Or they're already gone, and the trunks stand around naked, like weird, white sculptures. Whole hillsides look like boneyards. I've heard rumors that they'll all be gone within ten years. It looks like Dutch elm disease all over again, but this time the epidemic has hit a tree that means a lot more to me than any old elm.

Maybe more than any other species, the paper birch represents the north country. With its smooth, white, useful bark, the birch is as exotic, in its way, as the palm tree or the baobab. Wherever birches grow, I tend to feel at home. And so it grieves me to see them going down in such devastating numbers. A recent drive through Superior National Forest upset me so much I called the Department of Natural Resources. A friendly forester said no, I wasn't seeing things. The birches *are* dying, for a variety of reasons. Drought in the late eighties weakened the trees, making them especially vulnerable to insects, the worst of which is the bronze birch borer. But mostly, he told me, the birches are simply dying of old age. It's been about a century since the virgin pines were cut and birches sprang up in softwoods were felled birches grew up and still flourish, touch wood.

But why are they white? And why am I so glad to see them? It must have something to do with the snow. Perhaps it's protective coloration. After all, it's winter here seven months out of the year. When the weather gets cold the ptarmigan turns white, and so does the snowshoe hare. Think of polar bears. And the Finns, in World War II, they only had rifles and skis, but they dressed in white clothes, and they held off the whole Russian army for weeks. So maybe that's why birch trees are white.

But why am I so glad to see them? I don't understand it, but birch trees are kind of like women to me: they make me excited and peaceful. When I drive past a stand of birches, it's as if I'm driving by a hospital just as a whole flock of nurses are getting off work. I look and look. And all of these wonderful women I see, they don't care about me, but they make me feel lucky to be here. If you get up close to a birch tree you notice the bark isn't white after all but silver, pale green, pink, and blue. Nothing is simple, neither peace nor love nor the color of birch trees. As I write these words down on white paper, paper made out of wood, Finland is peaceful, Russia is calling its armies home, Sweden is peaceful, Norway, Denmark, the States, Canada, the entire domain of the birch is at peace. And if you stretch out under a birch with someone you love — or even someone you like a little — you can feel, for a minute or two, the great calm under all things, the peace so profound it passes all understanding.

their place. Many of these trees are past maturity, so
they're dying now, to be replaced, in the natural order
of things, by maple and basswood or, more commonly
up here, spruce and balsam fir. Birches regenerate
strongly, sending up shoots from stumps and roots, so
they're not about to disappear completely, the forester
assured me. But we're not going to see them anymore
in the glimmering profusion we'd grown used to. And
that's a sadness, which won't be wiped away by talk
about the evolution of the forest or natural succession.

I wrote a prose poem a while back, intended then as
a celebration of the birch, but which may finally have
to serve as a sort of elegy.

Why Birch Trees Are White

I've seen thousands, millions by now, and still they
amaze me. On hot, sticky days their trunks remind me
of columns of snow, and the green froth of their foliage
is also refreshing. In winter they fit with the snowscape
or stand out from the boring background of popple and
brush like those people at parties you want to meet
right away.

Birches were to the Ojibway what buffalo were to
the Sioux. They used them for wigwams, baskets,
canoes. . . . Those trees are still with us, but look at the
poor buffalo. Slaughtered by whites by the millions.
Buffalo traveled in gigantic herds and raised a real
ruckus, not to mention the dust. But birches were too
tough to eat, and they didn't make such a fuss. They
kept quiet and stayed in one place. There might be a
lesson in that. Even though the giant red and white
pines have gone the way of the buffalo, where the

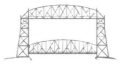

Family Car Camping

Although my family did a lot of car camping when I was a boy, I turned my back on that activity once I hit my twenties. By then I was going out with the guys, exploring the border lakes by canoe, and this kind of camping was so clearly superior, so much more primal, I decided I'd never camp out of a car again except as a cheap alternative to staying in a motel. I was a proud young buck in those days, and car camping — with park stickers and Coleman stoves and noisy neighbors — struck me as pathetic, something for middle-aged fat guys with families.

Well, I'm no longer young or slim, and I seem to have picked up a family. The age and girth came naturally over time; the family I acquired by falling in love with the divorced mother of two young girls. All three of these ladies like the outdoors, but at first the girls were too little to appreciate portages or paddle through whitecaps. And so I found myself, quite suddenly, in the dreaded category of family car camper.

For our initial outing, we decided to try a couple of nights at Sioux Narrows, up on the east side of Lake of the Woods. I love Ontario. It's just like Minnesota, only more so. Our decision to camp in Canada proved intelligent, because the traffic thinned out once we crossed the border. We helped ourselves still more by going early in the week, so we were able to avoid the fierce, ratlike competition for campsites that commonly occurs in Minnesota state parks. I was also relieved that the noise level remained relatively low throughout our stay. I have dreadful memories of family car camping expeditions ruined by radios, TVs, hot rods, and obnoxious midnight revelry. But our neighbors at Sioux Narrows were nicely subdued. Maybe it was the influence of those signs you find in provincial parks, signs that make my poor heart lurch with incredulity and joy: "NO EXCESSIVE NOISE at any time." I know I'm in a foreign country when I see those signs, because most Americans believe they have a God-given right to raise a racket. And if, by accident or law, such a sign were erected in an American park, it wouldn't be half so polite. It would only command QUIET! or shout NO NOISE! But the Canadians, God bless them, give you a little essay on a post: "NO EXCESSIVE NOISE at any time." Charming. Still, car camping can't provide the peace of deep woods solitude. Most of the drawbacks I remembered remained. Just as you're drifting off to sleep, savoring the distant yodel of a loon, the headlights of a latecomer flash through your tent, and the car growls past, engine thrumming, tires crunching gravel. Morning and evening, motorboats buzz, annoying as bumblebees. Our particular campsite was troubled by a

couple of chipmunks so confident of their cuteness
they were constantly underfoot. And sure enough, our
youngest went soft and insisted on feeding them half
our groceries. At such times I want to adopt a boy, one
of my own kind, who when he sees "Chippy" doesn't
think cuddle but kill. Then there was the wet slabwood
provided by the park — for which they expect you to
pay! — chunks of green junk that made me sputter
with exasperation when I tried to cut the stuff, wishing
I were twenty and alone, fifty miles from anywhere and
free to choose my own damn wood.

In my more realistic moments, though, I remembered this car camping trip wasn't mainly for me but
the kids . . . and the girls were having a high old time —
catching crayfish with raisins for bait, swimming with
Indian kids off the nearby reserve, shining flashlights
through their fingers at night and scaring each other
with spider stories. Wasn't that why we'd come — to
give them some fun and make a few memories? They
already had plenty to take from this trip: how I paddled
the canoe all of one morning searching for fish but got
skunked, only to find their mother had caught two fat
bass just by casting off of the dock; how the oldest,
complaining of thirst in the dark, was handed the
wrong plastic bottle and drank dish detergent; how the
youngest, goofing around, tripped and fell full-length
in the lake. Memorable, laughable moments all.

As someone who has only taken on parental duties in
middle age, I'm still stunned, sometimes, by the amount
of effort and self-sacrifice required to create those
memorable moments. More than once, when the kids
were whining like giant mosquitoes and I had to put off

my own desires, I wondered what the hell I was doing
there, camping out of a car, for Chrissake. It helped to
remember my own parents then and recall our smelly
old green canvas tent and the air mattresses that always
collapsed and how my folks did almost all of the work
while I ran off and played. Lying in my sleeping bag on
our final night at Sioux Narrows, I remembered how
my parents took us kids and pitched camp at
Whitewater State Park even there at the end of my
mother's life, when Dad had to drive her in to the
Mayo Clinic for regular cancer treatments. I lay there
in the dark and thought about my parents lying in the
dark some thirty years before. What conversations they
must have kept from us. What thoughts they must have
thought. What anguish the very sight of us kids must
have caused. But I saw precious little of that. What
I saw, come daylight, was fire crackling in the grate and
my father standing at the Coleman stove, frying bacon.
When I woke the last morning at Sioux Narrows,
I stepped out of the tent and gazed back through the
screen at the three human beings I cared about most —
one big, one little, one in between, each of them snor-
ing at her own peculiar pitch. I thought, Hey. This is
okay. This is fun.

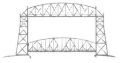

The Duluth behind Duluth

To love any particular place in this country is dangerous because most people don't, and when they do, they
do it badly. Look at the Black Hills. Look at Los
Angeles — if you can find it under the smog. Try visiting Yellowstone National Park. Go look for the prairie
in Eden Prairie.

To love any place in this country is dangerous
because you're almost certain to lose it. I'd wanted to
live in Duluth all my life, and my first two weeks in
town I was ecstatic. This was years ago, but I remember
having two clear thoughts in all that irrational happiness. My first thought was this was a place worth fighting for. My second thought was I needed another
Duluth, since I was bound to lose any such fight.

I didn't have to think very hard to realize I already
had a backup — in Houghton, Michigan. Some years
earlier I had visited the Keweenaw, that thumb of land
stuck in the belly of Lake Superior up there on the

Upper Peninsula. I had liked the town of Houghton instantly, and I was struck by the parallels to Duluth. Like Duluth, Houghton is built on a hill. Like Duluth, which has a twin in Superior, Wisconsin, Houghton has a poor sister city in Hancock. Ore boats pass through the ship canal that separates Houghton from Hancock, and the two towns are linked by a bridge that lifts. No wonder I felt at home. Today when I worry that Duluth may be transmogrified into a nautical theme park featuring water bikes and helicopter rides, a dismal Disneylake of the North, it's a comfort to remember Houghton-Hancock.

Of course, it takes a peculiar person to take comfort in the thought of Houghton-Hancock. We're talking about a depressed region that gets hit with such heavy snowfalls that people build docks out from their houses rather than sidewalks. We're talking about a town where the chief tourist attraction is an abandoned mine shaft. Still, there are those of us who simply can't resist a gritty city in a pretty setting. I recall a conversation I had a few years back with Anthony Bukoski, who has written splendid stories about the rust and despair of Superior, Wisconsin, and with Tony's cousin, who escaped to California long ago. Tony's cousin is the kind of guy who regularly flies his own plane to Monterey for lunch. But every now and then he comes back to Duluth-Superior for laughs. He was laughing that night, hunched over his drink in the dark of Frankie's Tavern, dressed in a brown leather jacket and a white silk scarf, exclaiming with incredulity: "This town is a museum! This is the only city in the country where people still keep track of their change. This is the only place I know where I can watch an old lady at the checkout counter squeezing her little plastic coin purse. This is the only city on earth where people think their heating bills are a fit topic for conversation. Talk about the end of the line! I don't think there's a more provincial, benighted place in America — unless maybe it's Houghton, Michigan."

"Great town!" Tony and I declared in unison.

"Sweet spot."

"Oh, yeah, terrific city."

The cousin shook his head and bought us each another drink, dismayed by our perversity.

To appreciate places like Duluth-Superior and Houghton-Hancock, you need a hot streak of scorn for what's fashionable and profound affection for what's been wrecked and overlooked. One reason I love the U.P. is that it's already been abandoned by the megamachine of American capitalism. Logged off and mined in the nineteenth century, the Keweenaw is haunted by ghost towns and ghost homesteads, slagheaps and cellarholes, apple trees run wild. The pines are growing up again, the scarred landscape is slowly healing over, but everywhere you go there are ruins to remind you of human arrogance and failure. This is exactly what the sanitary suburbs lack. I always feel encouraged when I visit such a busted region. Here's a place, I think, where people aren't so likely to buy the lies of government and business. Here's a place where people have to keep the past in mind.

My wife and I chose the U.P. for our middle-aged, prenuptial honeymoon. The ruins of the Keweenaw seemed an appropriate setting, since we both had broken

marriages behind us. We found bed and breakfast in
a partially restored Victorian mansion originally built
by the owner of a copper mine. Delighted to have the
run of his house, I half expected to glimpse the ghost of
an overdressed lady in the huge hallway mirror, to hear
laughter left over from the past century issue from the
attic ballroom. We slept, my love and I, in a bedroom
that was plenty large enough for us but had only served
the original owner as his cedar closet. The room had
been carefully constructed to keep out moths and all
manner of corruption, but the fancy suits and gowns
were long gone now, the rich man himself gone into
the ground, and it was richly satisfying to contemplate
that rich man's end and see how the home of that
expert exploiter of others had been opened to the hoi
polloi at last. The red cedar walls and ceiling of our
room had grown silvery with age, and it was lovely to
lie there, deep in love, a little silvery ourselves but
warm and lively still, breathing the sweet aroma of that
room. Such pleasures require a certain amount of history, some seasoning and character, something unavailable to fresh young couples at the Holiday Inn.

But beyond its broken, tragic atmosphere, I love the
U.P. because it feels so much like home. At a time when
everyone seems to be tripping off on a prestige vacation to New Zealand or Tibet, I'd rather not compete.
Travel to foreign countries always feels sort of sad and
voyeuristic to me anyhow. To truly enjoy a place and
feel I've got the right to be there, I have to be able to
imagine myself living there. That's easy for me on the
U.P. Basically, it's the same as northern Minnesota, with

just enough variation to make things interesting.
Instead of a rocky, rugged shore on Lake Superior,
they've got heaps of sand. Instead of iron, they've got
copper. Raspberries give way to thimbleberries over
there, and Swedish names are overwhelmed by Finnish
and Italian. It's fun to see so many signs that end in
"ainnonen" or "inni." And the cuisine is just exotic
enough to let you know you're somewhere else. Pasties,
the miner's lunch of chopped meat and vegetables
baked inside a crusty envelope, can be found in almost
any town. I saw codfish eggs and potatoes offered on a
breakfast menu. The Kaleva Cafe in Hancock was serving two items I'd never heard of — loaf soup and nisua.

The differences between the Upper Peninsula of
Michigan and Minnesota's Arrowhead keep me interested, but the similarities put me at ease. It's the attitude
of the "yoopers," as residents of the U.P. call themselves — it's their bad attitude, as much as anything,
that lets me feel at home. This odd outlook includes
the idea that berrypicking, saunas, and deer hunting
may be more important than full-time employment.
Then there's their healthy antagonism toward the
southern, urban part of the state. This is far stronger on
the U.P. than the bad-ass posture Rangers take toward
Minneapolis. For a while, the yoopers even talked
about seceding. But best of all, the yoopers exhibit a
sense of irony about themselves that feels to me both
familiar and almost fatally seductive. Several years ago,
when the state adopted the rather dopey slogan "Say
Yes! to Michigan," bumper stickers appeared all over
the Upper Peninsula that read, "Say ya to da U.P., eh?"

I'm glad to know I've got a home away from home, so that when the day comes that Duluth is finally destroyed by discount malls and tourism — or terrorism, as we often call it here — I'll still have a place to hide out. When dat day comes I tink I say ya to da U.P., eh?

Emil's Place

Every other summer I spend some time up at Lake of the Woods, where my wife still owns, with her ex, a picturesque, ramshackle farm. I'm always reluctant to leave Duluth, but my wife's history on the farm reaches back a quarter century, and the kids keep some of their earliest memories there. Who am I to deny them?

Life on the farm is primitive but peaceful. We pump and carry water to the house in white enamel pails. On rainy days we fire up the barrel stove to drive off the chill. There's a flashlight by the door for trips to the outhouse at night and a badminton racket beside the bed to whack any bats that trouble our sleep. We rent the fields to genuine farmers and just barely manage, ourselves, to keep the grass cut, the dead trees cleared, the buildings in decent repair. For entertainment, we bang the old upright piano, pick berries, hunt mushrooms, fish the bay for northerns, soak up sun at the white sand beach, and drive the backroads with an eye out for wildlife and stories.

The stories are everywhere, even though the population is sparse up there on the border. Maybe that empty landscape makes the local folks look larger than the ordinary run of human beings. Maybe people brood and talk about each other more when there are fewer of them. Or maybe I'm just seeing things through the eyes of my wife, who has a powerful appreciation for those cockeyed, colorful people we call "characters" — as if they belonged in a book, as if their stories demanded to be told. At any rate, Lake of the Woods County — one of the last to be settled, one of the poorest in the state — seems unusually rich in remarkable people. Down the road a piece, there's a dairy farmer who buys most of his groceries off a truck because he thinks the merchants in town are nothing but a bunch of pirates. He doesn't own a telephone because it's too expensive and, besides, who'd want to call *him*? Closer to home, there's a young fellow who's been trying for several years to order himself a bride through the mail. Just across the creek lives an old lady who still farms her place alone. The sign at the end of her driveway welcomes visitors with this warning: Not Responsible For Accidents.

Each of these people is worthy of a full-fledged biography. But the person who haunts me most is a man I never met, a man I'm going to call Emil Olson. My wife had mentioned him several times, but I never paid any special attention until the day she came into the house and announced, "I stopped over at Emil Olson's place." She seemed calm but softened somehow, and

I saw that she'd been deeply moved. Emil had died the year before, and she told me how she'd walked around his place back there in the jackpines, and what she'd seen, and how she'd sat down in the yard and cried, thinking not only of Emil but of several other old bachelors in the area, too, and how they'd died off one by one. Emil's friend Johnny had hung himself in his basement. Another old guy in town had hung himself from a willow tree. Such a stark end to these solitary lives. It was horrifying. It was grievous. It made the world seem cold as outer space.

I've always been touched by my wife's tenderness toward these old geeks. I suppose it's the old man in me, responding gratefully to such affection from a woman in her prime. But my wife was so . . . I don't know . . . so kind of *shy* about Emil's place in the woods, it was clear she thought of it as sacred ground. A few days later I asked if she would take me there.

The land around Lake of the Woods is not especially scenic. It runs toward bog and hayfields, scrapwoods and brush. But here and there a sandy jackpine ridge rises out of the lower ground, and Emil's place was located on one of those. We drove in past a gravel pit, and then the dirt road wound around through the trees. We drove across a cable lying in the road, and then we came out in a sunshot clearing in the pines. There stood the house and a small, two-story barn, and a long, open shed. My wife said, "He used to keep that cable strung across the road, so you'd have to park and walk up to the house. He'd hear you coming and sneak around through the woods and walk up behind you, take you by surprise. It was creepy."

Emil was a nut, of course. I knew the type. In the tiny towns where I grew up, there always seemed to be at least one of these lonely men living on the fringe of the community — ragged, poor, and vaguely angry. Such men were often both oddly religious and para- noid. Their sexuality was ambiguous, and our parents warned us away from them. They made their living catch-as-catch-can, and frequently they knew impor- tant secrets — where to dig ginseng or pick wild mush- rooms, how to snag walleyes or handle snakes. As kids we were both frightened and attracted by these charac- ters, and we honored such a man by giving him a title. Instead of calling him by name, we'd refer to him as The Hermit.

Clearly, Emil had been worthy of that appellation. My wife had shown me an old newspaper clipping in which Emil had advertised his work as a handyman. The ad closed with The Hermit's typical note of para- noia: "Those who have spoken ill of me need not apply." But even paranoids have enemies, and this seems to be especially true of hermits. Their very suspicious- ness generates the enemies they've imagined. True to type, Emil Olson had attracted petty persecution. His enemies — probably teenage boys, terrified of The Hermit in themselves — had tampered with his mail and beat up on his mailbox. My wife had a daffy story about the deputy sheriff coming out and making plaster casts of footprints around Emil's mailbox. She had also seen old letters in which Emil expressed his deep belief in the wickedness of women. And yet in his late old age, Emil had developed a kind of crush on a young, married neighbor woman. The odd form his affection took was that every day he waited by her mailbox to prevent anyone from messing with her letters. He'd collect her mail himself and deliver it by hand. So you'd pass this woman's driveway, and there sat Emil, crouched in his car, sweet and crazy, guarding the mailbox of his beloved.

Hermits are eccentric. They're just like us but different. That's what fascinates us. I felt like an archaeologist as my wife and I explored Emil's clearing in the woods. He'd chosen a lovely place for his homestead, but the signs of his eccentricity showed up even in the yard. Here, for example, was his motor scooter, the very peculiar vehicle he had driven before he could afford the Plymouth, which rested, now, without wheels or windows, up on blocks nearby. The scooter seemed to be built from steel he'd hacked off a bedframe. The motor was out of a washing machine, the wheels had come off a lawn mower, and it had a chunk of sofa for a seat. The whole contraption was fastened together with nuts and bolts. This was Emil's patented method of construction. Homemade wagons and furniture were scattered around the yard, all of them stuck together with nuts and bolts. The man enjoyed making things. Why in hell hadn't he learned how to weld?

It was the interior of the house, however, that moved me most. A pair of signs in the entryway, scrawled in blue ballpoint, showed that Emil was a lot like us and had, in fact, expected company. One sign said, "I'm down in the garden." The other declared, "I'm out cutting wood." But Emil was different, too. He'd never taped or painted his sheetrock, for example, and the raw walls of his house were filthy with soot. What really struck me, though, was Emil's furniture. I wasn't surprised to see that Emil had chosen a carseat for his sofa, but this particular piece of furniture bore the distinctive mark of Emil's ingenuity. He'd made a frame for the carseat and mounted it on lawn-mower wheels so he could move it easily around the house. And then there was the stump stool. This was nothing but a rusty tractor seat nailed to a chunk of wood. Apparently, this had been Emil's kitchen chair. As my wife and I moved through the barren rooms, examining these artifacts, we murmured when we spoke at all. We might have been exploring an Egyptian tomb. But there was no gold here. Only broken crockery, blackened silverware, musty magazines. Bible verses were taped to the walls. A sign above the stove said, "God Loves You."

As I stepped outside in the sunlit yard, I felt numb with grief and wonder. If God loved Emil Olson, why had he been given such a dirtpoor, lonesome life? Then I saw my wife carrying Emil's stump stool to the car. "I'm taking this," she said. "I want to have something to remember him by."

Back home in Duluth, she set up the stump stool in the garden, where it made a place to take a break from bending over plants, to pause and watch the passing clouds, to give a thought to Emil. In winter, we move the stool inside, where it makes a handy spot to sit and pull on boots or set things down when we come in. And it serves as a daily reminder of Emil's sunlit clearing in the woods.

Not that I really need one. Emil's place has cleared a space inside my head. It's a psychological hermitage, and I go there every day to be alone. I try not to worry about this. After all, it's not just crazy people who value solitude but saints and artists, too. Christ Himself withdrew from the multitudes to meditate and pray. The urge to be alone may only look crazy to us because *we're* insane, addicted to hubbub and yakkety-yak.

Emil's place quiets me. I'm always glad to go there, however sad it makes me. I tour the barren house once more, walk down through the meadow where Emil kept his garden, peek inside the pumphouse maybe, maybe look inside the barn. Then I drag the stump stool out in the yard. I am deeply pleased to be here, simply to sit and contemplate the lonesome, enigmatic life of Emil Olson. Emil's life was a joke, and yet there's a mystery here, some terrible, irreducible dignity I cannot understand. I cannot understand it. Sunlight pours over my head until my hair feels hot, as if I might catch fire. The air is heavy with the sweet perfume of jackpines. I throw my head back and look up, beyond the treetops, at the heavens, which are beautiful, pure blue, and absolutely empty.

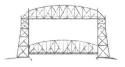

Blueberry Country

Lately I've been wondering how on earth I ever forgot about blueberries. When I was a kid on the Canadian border, blueberries held a humble but respected place in the local economy, and, for a brief period each year, darkened every mind and tongue in the township. When I look back through the lens of memory, those little sky-blue berries loom as large as grapes. But my family moved away, and I grew up, and blueberries became another pricey product in the supermarket, too expensive for my pocketbook, and flavorless compared to the wild fruit I'd eaten as a boy. Though I've been back in blueberry country for some time now, I've seldom given blueberries a thought, but recently two things — an afternoon on Madeline Island and a book of poems — conspired to remind me what I'd lost.

The book of poems is called *A Field Guide to Blueberries*. It's by my friend Jim Johnson of Duluth, and it's a daffy, whimsical, observant, thoughtful little volume. It's about blueberries, all right, but many other things besides, touching myths and legends, telling bits of stories, including comments on the jackpine culture of northern Minnesota. This poem may be my favorite in the book.

> *In Isabella, Minnesota, I Have Found Crystals*
> *of Dirty Snow under a Log, Even in July*

And blueberries
  green blueberries, red blueberries, ripe blueberries
  blue blueberries, blueberries blue as Finland
  blue-black blueberries, black-blue blueberries
  white-spotted blueberries, withered white
  blueberries, thousands and thousands of
  blueberries — each one the end of summer.

Having browsed through Jim's book several times, I had blueberries on the brain when I set out with my family on a recent trip to Madeline Island. On the way, we passed through the tiny town of Blueberry, Wisconsin. I took it as a sign. This was basically a camping trip to entertain the kids, but I also had in mind a mile and a half of brown sand beach on Madeline Island where I'd seen blueberries before. Plenty of pickers had preceded us and thinned the patch, but there was still a sprinkling of blue beneath the pines. Dorothea scoffed when I selected a two-quart stainless steel saucepan as my berry bucket. She's spent two dozen summers up at Lake of the Woods, and she told me the blueberry ladies of Baudette wouldn't be caught dead with such a heavy unit. "For casual picking like this, it's always a plastic sack," she said, stuffing one in her pocket.

"And what do they use for a serious assault?" I asked. I remembered a coffee can fixed up with a wire handle as the classic choice.

"Plastic ice cream pails," she said, and I realized I was a hopeless amateur — nostalgic, romantic, out of touch.

Nonetheless I insisted on my metal pan, braving my wife's ridicule for the sake of that faint, soft music I remembered from my youth and heard again as I dropped the first few berries in the pan: *ping, pong, ding, dang, dong.*

As we worked down the backbone of the beach, the sun, the wind, the peppermint scent of the pines, the very act of bending to the berries, all combined to start a memory slideshow flashing in my head. I saw purple syrup; purple sauce; big farm women serving pie that oozed a hot, sweet, purple goo; bowls of berries black as night, swimming in raw cream, twinkling with sugar grains. And I recalled a family photograph taken almost forty years ago. My father's brothers had come visiting, and he'd guided them across the border to his special spots. They'd found the mother lode, and they stand there in the snapshot like hunters with their trophies, their smiles broad and brilliant, their white shirts blinding in the sun, each of them extending proudly in his arms a peach crate heaped with wild berries. I know those men. They're gray and trembling now, nearing death, each of them. Yet they stand there, young and strong, in my mental picture of that photograph, making this grand gesture of abundance.

Oh, it was a strange, extravagant harvest I gathered there on Madeline. The actual, edible berries may have been the least of it, though I delighted in that lowly fruit, round and blue as the globe on which it grows. I'd recovered a family tradition I meant to carry on. I'd missed high season this year, but that was a mistake I would not make again.

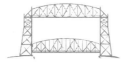

Eating the Landscape

Henry David Thoreau, that visionary crank, said he went to the woods in order to live deliberately. I go to the woods to get lost. Deliberately. On purpose. Oh, I usually reach my destination all right. I seldom have to consult my compass. I don't mean that. I mean that I go to the woods in order to lose my everyday social self — to just drop it — as a buck drops his antlers or a snake sheds his skin. I want a new self, a new world. Or an ancient one. And so I go to the woods — for an hour or two or for days at a time — in order to be surprised. Some surprises are mild: the toad on the trail, the hawk overhead. But some are so severe I'm forced to rethink my life. There's nothing I like better than being so surprised I have to wonder, What on earth? Where am I? Who am I now?

I'd heard about the Superior Hiking Trail for several years, and I'd even bought a copy of the excellent guide published by the volunteers who built and maintain it.

But I'd only ever sampled the tiniest piece of the trail.
First and foremost, I'm a canoeist; I spend most of my
free time between ice-out and freeze-up paddling the
lakes of Minnesota's Arrowhead. Why would anyone
walk, I've always wondered, when you can float? But
I loved the idea of the Superior Hiking Trail. This
dreampath was conceived in the 1980s by a small group
of enthusiastic walkers who saw the possibility of con-
structing a footpath, modeled after the famous
Appalachian Trail, that would follow the ridgeline
above Lake Superior, 240 miles from Duluth to the
Canadian border. These people enlisted the help of
state agencies, persisted, and now the trail is almost
complete. What a wild idea. What a civilized notion.
What a sweet-scented dream come true.

On a Saturday near the end of summer, a day too
windy to canoe, I set out to try a section of the trail.
A fifty-minute drive up the North Shore brought me to
the mouth of the Split Rock River. The loop I planned
to hike, a four and a half mile walk up the river and
back, was supposed to be one of the best daytrips on
the entire trail.

I hoped the path wouldn't be too rough. As a novice
hiker, I hadn't invested in fancy footwear; my old running shoes would just have to do the job. I slipped into
my overstuffed daypack and grabbed my fishing rod
out of the trunk. I knew there'd be pools along the
river, and every North Shore stream holds trout.
Besides, I'd been fishing all summer. I'd feel naked without my rod.

Before heading up the trail, I turned for a last look at
Lake Superior. The lake was both blue and silver today,

and the surface was broken with whitecaps. A big wind was blowing up out of the south, and huge rollers were crashing in the bay. As I stood gazing out at the greatest of all the Great Lakes, I remembered something I'd read recently about Indian women in the old days. In the old days, apparently, Ojibway mothers used to take their children to the lakeshore, point, and tell them, "There is your real mother. I am just a substitute." What a lovely thing to do, I thought, and I wished, wistfully, that my own mother had told me some such thing before she'd died back when I was young. I turned, and plunged into the woods.

After a ten-minute climb through popple and birch, I reached the main trail. I turned down into a dark, sun-shot ravine and crossed a small tributary of the river. A waterfall made white noise upstream while, down below, the creek curved close to the rockface where water had carved a kind of cave. A couple was camped here in the shadows, their damp clothes strung out on a line to dry.

Huffing, I climbed the ridge above the ravine and then, descending toward the Split Rock River itself, looked down on a broad set of rapids and a chute of whitewater that went rocketing around the bend. I moved down to the stream and stepped out on the redrock riverbed that seemed, like the water, to be flowing downhill. A fisherman was working the black pool below the rapids. Clearly, this was not undiscovered country. But how could I complain? I peeled off my sweaty shirt, sat down, and lit up a small cigar.

I can't say how long I sat there, but I know I was happy, listening to the thunder of the river, soaking up sunlight. Like nearly everyone up here in the north, I live with an almost constant angst, even at the bright height of summer, unable to escape the heavy knowledge that winter is on the way. And so, like a lazy snake, I luxuriated in the sunshine before heading on up the trail. As I walked, I noticed with dismay that the ferns were already turning brown and the flowers of autumn had come. The asters that lined the footpath like little lavender daisies could only mean one thing — the snows were coming . . . and the end of the world was coming.

But how could I complain? Hiking the Split Rock trail was like walking through a book of Eliot Porter photographs. I saw so many waterfalls I quit keeping count. Cascades and rapids sparkled in the sun. Every bend in the river revealed raw rhyolite, volcanic rock so red it looked like the flesh of the earth. Near the top of the trail, I was startled by a pair of redrock pillars, two free-standing chimneys, like one of those weird formations found in the desert Southwest. Yet here they stood, as real as rock, deep in the green of the lush northwoods.

At the top of the trail, where a wooden footbridge crosses the river, I paused to eat lunch and check out the campsites. I also removed the official logbook from its little wooden house and glanced through the entries. A man named Andy claimed that he was in heaven. "After I die," someone from Indiana had written, "I hope I get to live on this trail forever." Hiker's hyperbole, I smiled to myself. But I knew how they felt. I was having a hard time keeping my own feet on the ground.

As I started down the far side of the stream, I discovered a campsite with views that resembled scenes from an ancient Chinese painting. But then the trail veered away from the river, and I was walking down a hallway through the trees. Enclosed by foliage, I grew broody and felt a cloud of autumnal desperation pass over me again. The school year was coming on, and the kids' activities were heating up. A long list of fall chores scrolled through my head—pick the apples, dig the spuds, paint the fence, restack the wood. And somehow I'd have to make the time to visit my dad.

My father was fading, and I didn't see him often enough. Nearly eighty now, he'd grown foggy with Alzheimer's over the past dozen years. He still had long moments of lucidity, but then, without warning, he would lose his bearings. The last time my sister had visited, she'd asked if he knew who she was, and he'd told her, "Sure. You're Santa Claus." Old age was funny, wasn't it? Funny and sad. And here was goldenrod beside the trail, and pearly everlasting, to remind me that another year was passing at this very moment, and I was aging, too.

My dad had undergone cancer surgery this past winter, and I'd felt certain he would die. But he'd survived, with the best possible prognosis. To everyone's surprise, he was up and wanting to take long walks within a week. Now *there* was a walker, I thought, and I laughed out loud. My father had grown up around Detroit Lakes, Minnesota, so he should have been a hunter or a fisherman. But he wasn't interested in killing things. He just liked to walk and watch the birds, enjoy the trees, notice any animals that came along.

A couple of summers back, on a visit down in Iowa, I had asked my dad about his life. "So, Pop," I said, "what are you up to these days? What are you doing with yourself?"

"Not so much," he mumbled. He considered the issue for a while. "Well, I do the dishes," he said finally. "I try to help out." We suffered through a long silence, but suddenly he brightened and said loudly, almost shouting in my face, "I like to walk! I like to walk a lot. I walk around town, quite a ways, a couple times a day. I really like it. Of course," he frowned, "it's hard in winter. This past year especially. So much ice and snow. I couldn't get out, I couldn't walk." He shot me a desperate look. "So finally I started walking in the basement."

"What?"

"I started walking in the basement. I cleared away some things down there, so I had a good path and I could walk around the furnace. Round and round." He snorted. "It's not the same, of course. But at least I could walk. That's what I do," he declared, giving me a triumphant stare, knowing he'd found the proper answer to my question. "I walk. I walk a lot."

I sat transfixed, shocked by the fierceness in my father's face.

"I walk," he said. "I walk, I walk, I walk."

So that was what I was doing here, I realized, hiking the Split Rock River Trail. I was following in my father's footsteps, even though he lived hundreds of miles away and had never ventured down this particular path.

I hadn't seen a soul in over an hour, so I was startled when a young backpacker appeared before me on the trail. We exchanged greetings and congratulated ourselves on the brilliant weather. And then he asked about the fishing. I stared at the fishing rod clutched in

my right hand. "Oh, this," I laughed. "I haven't taken
the time. Some other day, I guess." As I moved off
down the trail, I felt a little silly but soothed myself by
misquoting the Bible, mumbling beneath my breath,
"My rod and my reel, they comfort me."

I trudged along in a melancholy mood, preoccupied
with thoughts about my father. The air seemed thick
with sorrow and green shadows. But then I broke out of
the trees and followed the trail along the ridge, and
there was Lake Superior — wide as all the world, bluer
than the sky. The wind off the lake was exhilarating.
I paused to absorb the view and suck in oxygen. And
then I noticed that the ridgetop meadow was dotted
with bits of blue.

Berries. I hadn't found a decent patch of blueberries
all summer, but this one was huge. The berries beside
the trail were tiny and had plainly been picked over,
but back in the meadow they looked fat and plush.
Fumbling in my daypack for my cup, I waded out into
the patch. I popped a few berries in my mouth. My
God. What an ineffable flavor. They tasted like the
river, like the wind, like the sky.

The work was surprisingly slow, but, overcome by
a wave of gluttony, I picked as rapidly as I could. I was
running short of time today, but I promised myself I'd
be back tomorrow. My wife would be eager to come
along, and we'd bring a pair of plastic pails. To my con-
sternation, I noticed that my hands were trembling.
I was dropping half the berries I collected. So I sank to
my knees among the bushes and drew a deep breath.
What was going on here? Why was I feeling so
delighted — and so greedy?

Gradually, as I bent to the bushes, the sunshine burn-
ing my neck, it came to me. As much as I'd enjoyed the
hike, I'd felt oddly detached as I proceeded from one
scenic view to another — too much like a tourist with
a camera, who hurries from one photo op to the next.
The experience wasn't intimate enough. And then it hit
me. What I really wanted was to *eat* the landscape.
Wasn't that it? Yes, and these berries were giving me
my chance. Wasn't that it? Wasn't that why no canoe
trip felt complete until I'd caught, killed, cleaned,
cooked, and devoured a fish? That was it, all right.
I wanted to eat this country, to make it *mine*.

This realization was slightly frightening, but it didn't
stop me from picking berries as fast as I could. At bottom, I thought, I was a cannibal. This was the sort of
consuming desire an infant feels for its mother — sav-
age love; heinous hunger; pure, primal appetite. I went
on working in the light of this new knowledge, and,
from time to time, looked up from the small blue
spheres I cradled in my hand to the deep blue band of
Lake Superior stretched across the sky. The view was
a pleasure, and the shift in perspective made me somewhat giddy.

As I crawled through the bushes, I noticed with a
grin of satisfaction that my pants were stained with purple juice. So were my hands. I poured the berries into
my hat and dragged it along. I was down on all fours,
working in an ecstasy of greed and happiness.

And then a fly buzzed round my head. That familiar,
drowsy sound reminded me of how my father used to
take me berry picking way back in the bush when I was
little. I would pick enough fruit to darken the bottom of

my small, tin pail, but soon I'd grow lazy in the sun and fall asleep. And then, harassed by flies, I'd wake, not knowing where I was, and cry out for my dad, who, bending in the bushes, had disappeared from view. Now, more than forty years later, high above the Split Rock River and the infinite expanse of Lake Superior, glancing wildly around the empty meadow, I felt that same electric thrill of panic: Where's my father gone? *Dad?*

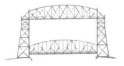

I Am Not a Duck Hunter

I was born to hunt. I've always loved the outdoors, and I spent the first six years of my life on the edge of the Roseau Wildlife Refuge, known in local parlance simply as The Bog. One Sunday morning when I was four, my parents left me with friends in a farmhouse beside The Bog while they went off to church. The women of the house entertained me in the kitchen and fed me my favorite breakfast—a thick slice of homemade bread doused with sugar and cream. I felt completely at home in that world of skirts and female laughter, fragrant steam rising from the cooking pots. But the peace was disturbed that morning when the men stomped in from The Bog. They were kind fellows, those farmers up there on the border, but still, they were men. They were big. They were gruff and slightly frightening. But I was fascinated by their gleaming guns, which they rested in a corner. They retired to the living room, and I remember very clearly sneaking in to take a good long peek at them. I know this is a knee-high memory, because I can't recall their faces at all. But I can see their giant bodies, dressed in brown, sprawling in the chairs. They had brought the raw odor of the open air inside the house, and blue smoke curled up toward the ceiling from their cigarettes. I was mightily impressed by their gear, the brassy glint of shotgun shells, the rubber squeak of their hip boots. These were men. Their voices rumbled. Some day I would be one of them.

By the time I was ten, the longing to hunt had grown acute. I read the outdoor magazines and fed my fantasies with the duck-and-dog novels for kids written by Jim Kjelgaard. But hunting tends to be a tradition that's passed from father to son, and my dad didn't hunt. My parents urged me to study nature instead. I remember how my hands trembled the day that package arrived from Montgomery Ward and I lifted out of their leather case my very own, very serious, very heavy 7 × 35 wide-angle binoculars manufactured by Bausch & Lomb. I ran right out to Miller's Hill, raised those big black glasses to my eyes, and beheld, at last, riding the muddy waters of the Des Moines River in flood, close-up, in color, the brilliant variety of the flyway: snows and blues and Canada geese, mallards and redheads and blue-winged teal, pintails, widgeons, and coots. I was electrified, and my excitement lasted a good ten years. For ten long years I was Adam in the garden all over again, satisfied to simply observe the creatures of this world and call them by their names. But that was a kind of hunting, too, for I kept lists, kept count. Rare species were my trophies, and I pursued them with a passion. As I crawled through muck and reeds to catch those feathered critters in my sights, I felt the hot surge of adrenaline, the fever of lust and greed, triumph, awe, and reverence — things a hunter feels — though I never fired a single shot.

The unfulfilled desires of youth often return in middle age. But I won't be going out to shoot ducks this fall, and I doubt that I ever will. I lost that aspiration because my parents pointed me in another direction that stopped short of blood sport but provided just as much excitement. And the hilarious satire about the duck hunting camp of Blackie LeVoy, which Jon Hassler wrote into his novel *The Love Hunter*, destroyed my romantic view of the sport forever. But the last vestige of my desire to drop ducks out of the sky expired one cold, gray morning several years ago when I saved a duck hunter's life.

At the time, I was living on Island Lake, outside St. Cloud, and I made it my practice that autumn to borrow my landlord's canoe and try for the nasty northerns that lurked in the cabbage weed. It was peaceful on that lake, with most of my neighbors gone off to work, and lovely to watch the season brighten and fade as the leaves lit up and then slowly, day by day, let go. I'd slip out every morning for an hour, and every third day or so, I'd catch a fish or two.

On this particular morning, I'd had no luck at all. I'd been fishing for an hour, but the lake seemed dead, and my fingers were stiff with cold. I was just about to head in when I heard a shotgun boom, and there, at the far, marshy end of the lake, something rolled and flashed in the gloomy autumn light like the belly of a giant fish — or, it struck me suddenly, the bottom of a boat. Then it was gone. I squinted, but I could see nothing down there, except, was that some sort of stick being waved in the air? A paddle? A gun?

I groaned with resentment — because I had work to do, because I was cold, because I only had a canoe. I didn't want to paddle the half mile down there for nothing and then have to fight my way back through the wind. So I almost went in, despite my peculiar vision. But then my Midwestern conscience — formed by years of Sunday school and the tales of rescue included in every issue of *Boy's Life* — my sluggish conscience, numbed by the cold, finally kicked in. Cursing, I picked up my paddle and turned the canoe toward the far end of the lake.

After a ten-minute paddle, I saw that I was in trouble. There was a man in the lake, thirty yards out from the marshy shore, in water up to his neck. How in the hell would I get him aboard? This weren't no broad-bottomed scow I commanded, but a skinny, tippy canoe.

It was very quiet out there, with no sound but the plash of my paddle as I approached the human head, which was topped by a canvas hunting cap.

The head spoke. "Good morning," it said.

"Good morning," I answered, "though in your case I guess that's more of a wish than a statement of fact."

The head smiled and said, "Help."

"I will," I said, "but I'm worried how we're going to manage this. What happened? Are you standing on the bottom?" I kept the canoe back a bit. I wasn't in any hurry. I didn't want the guy to come thrashing after me and tumble me into the water, too.

"I'm standing on my boat," he said. "Stupid," he said. "I lost my balance when I fired, and the bastard capsized. I couldn't swim with all these clothes on. I tried a couple times, but I kept sinking."

I had to admire this young man's cool. "Okay," I said, "I'll bring the canoe in, but please don't panic, or we'll both wind up in the drink."

"I know," he said. "It's cold. It's ice."

"I want you to come in over the bow. I'll try to counterbalance your weight."

As I brought the bow in close, the hunter raised one arm out of the water and dropped something heavy in the canoe. His gun. Then he got both hands on the gunwale, and I thought, This is it. "Careful," I snapped, and the hunter wrestled himself over the side as I leaned way back and made a tremendous wish.

Slopping aboard, the hunter heaved himself into the front seat. Water poured off his clothes. "That's better," he said. The canoe rocked wildly.

I steadied the boat and blew a big sigh.

"Thanks," the hunter said. "God, but I'm cold."

Turned out he was a college kid who lived just up the road. We traded names and information as we paddled back up the lake, and we shook hands once we'd beached the canoe.

"You okay?" I asked. He was shivering like crazy.

"Oh, yeah. Thanks again. I think you saved my life."

"Could be," I said, and I told him to take care.

A few hours later, I saw him running a motorboat down the lake with a friend. No doubt they meant to fish up his sunken duck boat. But oddly enough, I never saw that young man again. After all these years, I can't even remember his name. Was it Todd? Ted? I can't remember.

But I think of him often, especially in the fall. And even though I respect the ancient rites of hunting, and even though there's almost nothing I'd rather see in front of me than a plate of juicy duck, I can't forget how that young man looked as he clambered aboard my canoe. He looked like a drowned dog. And I guess that's why I don't hunt ducks.

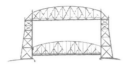

Lake Addiction

Novelist Fred Manfred wrote that we love a land-scape for the water it holds, and Norman Maclean declared at the end of *A River Runs through It* that he was haunted by waters. Those are both memorable state-ments—as clear and deep as Lake Superior—but I'm afraid my own relationship to water is more sinister. My name is Bart, and I'm a lakeaholic.

I counted up the other day and discovered that since I moved to Duluth, I have wet my canoe in two hun-dred different lakes. That figure does not include any water in Canada, Michigan, or Wisconsin, or even other parts of the state—just northeastern Minnesota. Nor does it count any repeat visits, of which there have been many. Two hundred lakes. That's about 20 new lakes a summer, or one new lake each week, which looks like I've got a problem.

Actually, to me, that figure seems low. This is sup-posed to be "the land of 10,000 lakes," but let's say

I limit myself to the Arrowhead region, which contains about a third of the water in Minnesota. Okay. That still leaves 3,000-some lakes, divided by twenty per summer, which means I'll have to live to be 150 years old in order to canoe them all.

How did I get caught by this compulsion anyhow? I didn't set out to be a lakeaholic. Isn't there someone I could blame? Well, sure. I could blame my brother, who took me out to a stupid bullhead pond one summer and got me hooked on fishing, which I had happily ignored till middle age. I could blame my dad, who caved in to my demands back in high school and drove me up to take a look at Ely, the gateway to canoe country. The way some alcoholics can recall their first drink with astonishing clarity, I remember stepping out of the car at the Kawishiwi River (which, I need to point out, is really a long string of lakes) and wandering down through the mossy, gray-green forest to gaze at the silver water dimpled with rain. But maybe it's not my father's fault. Maybe I should blame *his* father for settling near Detroit Lakes, out in the western part of the state. Or maybe I should go all the way back to the Old Country and place the blame on my Swedish ancestors, who were foolish enough to live on a beautiful island in the middle of Lake Siljan, completely unconscious of the voracious longing for water this would create in the souls of subsequent generations.

Oh, well. As any recovering addict knows, the idea is not to blame anybody but to find some way to live with the thirsty vampire inside. But maybe you're still not convinced there *is* such a thing as lake addiction. No? When I first moved to Duluth and asked about nearby spots where I could canoe, I was referred to a fellow named David Spencer. Spencer described several places where I could put in, and I learned that he kept his canoe on his car all through the summer. That way, he told me, he could always whip down to the harbor over his lunch hour, *in case he needed a quick fix*. That was his language. You think there's no such thing as lake addiction? One bright blue April morning, I saw Spencer and Sam Cook, outdoor writer for the *Duluth News-Tribune*, open the season by shoving a canoe out through the ice floes on Lake Superior. No such thing as lake addiction? One day in July I set out to do a little lazy fishing by myself. By day's end I had paddled five lakes and ten miles over twelve hours and caught nary one fish, though I did see a moose on the final portage, though I might have been hallucinating by then since I was shaking from exhaustion.

Of course there's such a thing as lake addiction. But one of the symptoms of this insidious disease is the deep need to deny you've got it. For years, for example, I swore I was only going fishing when I was actually indulging in lakeaholic behavior. If I were primarily interested in catching fish, no doubt I would simply squat for hours in a motorboat on one of the big walleye lakes just outside Duluth. But noooo. I have to start each trip by driving miles of gravel backroads deep into the woods in pursuit of a special experience even I can't define. No, no. In Minnesota, anyhow, fishing is a perfectly acceptable form of mental illness. But fishing is only a part of my problem.

This reminds me of a guy I know up in Ely who has broken through his denial. In private, among his own kind, he's willing to admit his overpowering need to canoe new lakes. But out there on the waterways, in public, he has to sneak and lie about it. He tells me he barely cares about fishing anymore, but every time he goes out for a paddle he makes damn certain he's got a fishing rod sticking up out of his canoe, as conspicuous as a car antenna, so his neighbors won't accuse him of having turned into some sort of fruitcake.

Another common symptom of lake addiction, besides the tendency to lie about the disease, is a powerful preoccupation with water. Daydreaming on the job, compulsive map reading, lingering overlong in the bathtub — all these are warning signs. The late great Irish poet William Butler Yeats identified the obsessive nature of the lakeaholic mind when he confessed that

> . . . always night and day
> I hear lake water lapping with low sounds by the shore;
> While I stand on the roadway, or on the pavements gray,
> I hear it in the deep heart's core.

Perhaps the most pathetic symptom of lake addiction, though, is the inability to stop after one or two lakes. Your normal social boater will be happy to paddle or put-put round the same pond all afternoon, even to fish the same stretch of water day after day through a two-week vacation. But the lakeaholic is always troubled by the thought that, as much as he's enjoying the way the sunlight glints off this lake, just over the ridge or just up the road, there's another lake, where the cliffs are higher, the trees are taller, the fish are fatter, and the water is — what? — wetter? Is that what he wants — wetter water? He can't say what he wants, but let's go. So he pulls out his boat and heads up the road long before he's finished exploring this lake, which, only the day before, he was dreaming of.

It was three summers back that I finally realized I was a junkie. I had fished a shallow lake for northerns in the morning, a deep trout lake at midday, and a lake with no name in the late afternoon. Now it was night. The sun was down. There was maybe an hour of after-glow left. I had hoisted the canoe on the car one last time, my body was aching, I had not caught one fish. And yet, when I spotted the sign to Eighteen Lake I hit the brakes. The cloud of dust I'd been raising enveloped the car. I coughed as I fought temptation but finally turned up the side road. How many times had I zoomed past that sign? Who knew what was in that lake?

The lake was absolutely lovely. The campground had red pines like gigantic pillars, the landing was an easy carrydown from the car, the water looked like molten copper. A loon cried as I launched the canoe, and I thought: This is what I've been looking for — the once-and-for-all-and-forever, positively perfect lake. All I needed now was fish. A few seconds later my fishing rod trembled, and I quickly reeled in . . . a two-inch perch. Which I quickly released. Then I caught a three-inch perch. Then another. And another. And another. Eighteen Lake was loaded with joke fish, little yellow perch the size of your thumb. I hauled the canoe from the lake, wrestled it onto the car, and drove off into the dark, quivering with shame and fatigue and the undeni-able knowledge that I was insane.

Life has grown easier since that evening of defeat and recognition. For one thing, I saw that I was pursuing an illusion. My personal survey of northeastern Minnesota is far from complete, but I've seen enough to conclude: There is no perfect lake, though nearly every lake has perfect moments. Such knowledge is profoundly helpful and can bring a lakeaholic days of peace. But, sad to say, there is no permanent cure for lake addiction. Otherwise why would I find myself rising in the cold November dark, swaddling my body in long underwear, gloves, and stocking cap, whispering: *"Somebody stop me."*

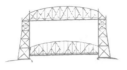

Epilogue

The Backroad to Ely

It's a cool, blue morning in June, and I'm sleepy but happy because I'm heading up to Ely for an overnight in the woods. I've got a neat, plump pack in the backseat, and the canoe is clamped like a cap to the roof of the car. It's 5:30 when I hit the expressway out of Duluth. The sun shines bright as a big brass gong as it breaks from the fog over Lake Superior.

A half hour up the North Shore, I stop in Two Harbors for an old-fashioned breakfast at Miller's Cafe — homemade hash browns, bacon and eggs. Plenty of cholesterol to carry me through the day. Crunching my crispy bacon strips, I brood over my dilemma. Since 1965 the Forest Service has required campers to obtain permits to enter the Boundary Waters Canoe Area. This measure is annoying but necessary in order to keep outdoors enthusiasts from loving the wilderness to death. You'd think a million acres would accommodate everyone, but the Boundary Waters has become the most popular wilderness area in the nation, and these days permits are often reserved months in advance — set aside by Boy Scout troops from Indiana, purchased by little old ladies from Tennessee, bought up in bunches by outfitters and resorts. This means that locals are frequently locked out of our own backyard, denied the possibility of spontaneous trips.

Here I sit, a case in point. I had hoped to camp on the Kawishiwi River tonight, but all four entry points were already reserved. Frustrated — and frustration runs high on this topic in northeastern Minnesota — I was forced to look for alternatives. So now I'm aiming for a lake just outside the Boundary Waters. Motors are permitted there, but this is a Wednesday, so I'm hoping for some quiet anyway.

At the edge of Two Harbors, I turn left on Lake County 2. This is the backroad to Ely, one of my favorite highways in the state. Most folks approach Ely by "the front door," shooting up U.S. 53, then cutting east on 169. That route makes sense; it's smooth and fast, with four wide lanes a good share of the way. But I've never cared much for common sense. I'll take Highway 2, with its dangerous ditches, lumps and bumps, and evergreens growing right up to the road. Over the years, I've become a connoisseur of roads. Lake County 2 is a good one.

On many maps this highway is only a thin gray line through the green of Superior National Forest. Sometimes it doesn't show up at all. Which makes it my kind of road. The first ten miles have been rebuilt in recent years, so I feel I'm cleared for takeoff and cruising down a runway. As the car climbs, I watch Lake

Superior fall away in the rearview mirror and merge with the sky. It's warmer over the hill, so I snap the heater off and crack the window. The car fills with the perfume of the forest — herbal, fresh, and sweet.

I first drove this road some thirty years ago, with an older cousin who went on to work as an ornithologist in Ecuador and Borneo. Northern Minnesota is exotic enough for me. Travel, they keep telling me, is broadening. But I don't want to be broad. I'm after depth. The brain insists on novelty, constant stimulation, but the soul desires the same old thing, renewed again and again. That's why I moved to Duluth ten years ago — to lose myself repeatedly in the woods and water of canoe country, to give myself some history here, to lay down layer upon layer of experience in the same old always different place. I won't see any tigers on this trip. I won't see anacondas. But I've seen bears on Highway 2. I've seen deer and moose. So, sleepy as I am, dreaming of cougars, I drive with one eye open for whatever actual wild thing may happen to appear. And, see? There's a ruffed grouse. There's a rabbit.

Halfway up Highway 2, the second-growth forest is darkened by a stand of white pines. From a distance, they resemble towering candelabras. These trees are so green they look black. Nothing says north like a white pine. Once upon a time, two hundred years ago, just the other day, white pines covered this entire region. It's a thought I can hardly bear to think. Today, less than 2 percent of the original forest remains. Somehow the loggers of the past century missed this particular stand, and, so far, the Forest Service has treated these trees with respect, creating a picnic area in their shadows,

sparing the giants that grow right next to the road,
tacking large reflectors to their trunks instead of sacrificing them for human safety and efficiency. I wind
through the pines in a matter of moments; but out in
the open again, whizzing through the scrapwoods,
I feel changed — haunted — as if I'd just awakened
from a disturbing dream about my ancestors.

For the most part, Highway 2 runs true as a ruler, so
I've been cheating the speed limit, racing down a long
green hallway. But now the forest walls flash open on
lakes and ponds and streams. There's Greenwood Lake,
where I stopped with my dad a quarter century back.
Sand River looks black this morning. And here's a
glimpse of Wampus Lake, a blue snapshot, perfect as an
ad for beer.

Highway 2 ends abruptly in a T with Highway 1.
I like these numbers — 1, 2. They're prime, like the
country they run through. Highway 1 is even more
attractive than Lake County 2. It's an impossible road,
careening like a roller coaster through the woods, guaranteed to cause carsickness in kids — which may
explain why the traffic is almost always light. Highway
1 makes me laugh every time I drive it.

I've been over this road so often by now I've nearly
got it by heart. Here's the Chub Lake Resort, battened
down and shuttered up, weathering into the ground.
The romantic in me loves these ruins — the wreckage
of some other person's dreams — and despises the glare
of success. So when will I learn, I suddenly wonder, to
honor my own disasters? Woops! Here's a logging
truck, and I swing way wide to avoid being smashed by

this mechanical dragon of the woods. The sign on the truck's bugscreen might be America's motto. EASY MONEY, it shouts. I laugh at my narrow escape and gun the car over the hill.

I'm told that people who like to read move more and more slowly down the page as they enter old age. With a lifetime of experience behind them and hundreds of books in their heads, every passage reminds them of some vivid incident out of their past, some other book they've read, and they wander off the page into alternative worlds of thought. That's how I feel about this wild highway. I'm reading the road like an old-timer, reminded of other days.

Here's the bend where, years ago, a friend and I helped a family put out a fire. And here's the bog where, just last week, my brother and I saw a big bull moose. Astonished, we stopped, amazed by his size and his calm demeanor as he stood there munching alder shoots. He was growing a new set of antlers, and his coat, this time of year, looked scruffy, as if he were made out of gunnysacks smeared with grease. But he was the rough, rude lord of these woods, and we were more excited than if we'd caught sight of the president.

Here's a backroad off the backroad — one of the best — and even as I flash past, speeding on up the asphalt toward Ely, I'm driving down the gravel to my favorite lake in this entire area. I'd tell you its name, but the word is Ojibway, and you wouldn't understand. A rough translation, though, would be Big Secret. Big Secret has never given me many fish, but it's just the right size for canoeing and offers the backdrop

I need—white pines, red pines, black spruce, white spruce, popple, birch, and cedar. One autumn day my wife and I took a break from fishing Big Secret and dragged our canoe up a granite slab. Coffee time. Then suddenly, out of nowhere, out of deep silence, came the howl of timber wolves: one voice at first—one long, lonely, wavering note—then several songs from other throats, twisting and twining around the first. My wife and I locked eyes, then gazed away at the green horizon. This music was more unearthly than Gregorian chant. Those animal voices rose and fell, quavered, and drifted away like smoke. The silence was deeper after they stopped. I looked at my watch. I'd waited thirty years to hear timber wolves howl, and their song had lasted less than three minutes. I felt like a mystic who had finally heard the voice of God. I was almost insanely happy, and yet, as we drove away from Big Secret that day, I felt more obsessed than before, determined that sometime I would see timber wolves in the flesh, as it were, in the fur.

I've got another lake in mind today, but, lost in these memories and reveries, I realize I may never make it to Ely. Still, that hardly matters anymore, because I'm getting what I wanted all along. Every trip I've taken up this backroad has been money in the bank, savings for my retirement. For soon the day will come when I'm too blind to drive, too creaky to canoe. But by then I won't need to leave the house. And when they lock me up in the nursing home, I'll slip off into the forest inside my own head. The Tibetans tell us this life is only a dream anyway, and the things that seem most real to us are dreams about our dreams. And so when the day arrives to make my final trip, I'll drive this backroad one last time, launch the canoe, and slide away on the silky water. The nurses leaning over my bed will be surprised by my smile and wonder aloud about my last words. "Was it *wolves*? I thought I heard him say *wolves*."

Permissions

The University of Minnesota Press gratefully acknowledges permission to reprint the following poetry in this book. Excerpts from "Terrible Weather Conditions," by John Engman, from *Temporary Help*, copyright 1998; reprinted by permission of the Estate of John Engman and Holy Cow! Press. Lines from "October Day," by Rainer Maria Rilke, translated by Robert Bly, from *Selected Poems of Rainer Maria Rilke*, published in 1981 by HarperCollins Publishers; reprinted by permission of HarperCollins Publishers. "Why Birch Trees Are White," by Barton Sutter, copyright 1993 by Barton Sutter, reprinted from *The Book of Names* with the permission of BOA Editions, Ltd., 260 East Ave., Rochester, NY 14604. "In Isabella, Minnesota, I Have Found Crystals of Dirty Snow under a Log, Even in July," by Jim Johnson, originally appeared in *A Field Guide to Blueberries*, by Jim Johnson, published by North Star Press of St. Cloud, Inc., in 1992; reprinted by permission of

the poet. Lines from "The Lake Isle of Innisfree," by
W. B. Yeats, are reprinted from *The Collected Works of
W. B. Yeats,* Volume 1: *The Poems,* revised and edited
by Richard J. Finneran (New York: Scribner, 1997);
reprinted with permission of Scribner, a division of
Simon & Schuster.

Barton Sutter is the author of *My Father's War and Other Stories* and *The Book of Names: New and Selected Poems,* both of which won Minnesota Book Awards. He has written for public radio, and his work has appeared in dozens of magazines, including *The Boundary Waters Journal, Minnesota Monthly,* and *Mpls.-St. Paul.* He teaches at the University of Wisconsin-Superior. A resident of Duluth since 1987, he has explored the canoe country of northern Minnesota for a quarter century.